学诚大和尚

Ven. Master Xuecheng

学诚大和尚侧记

Stories of Ven. Master Xuecheng

释慧空 著
Shi Huikong

中国物资出版社

Preface

As early as in 2006, Longquan Monastery was known to me as a Buddhist temple seated upon Fenghuangling (the Phoenix Ridge), part of Beijing's West Mountains. I had not had a chance to visit it until 2008, when I was taken there by one of my former students, a devoted volunteer of the Monastery, to attend its unforgettable yearly Moon Festival which greatly moved me. It was with this experience that I came to have a bond with Buddhism and Buddhists.

In 2009, the Translation Center of Longquan Monastery invited me to the Monastery to teach a course in English Linguistics for a group of its young volunteer translators. To my surprise, I found the volunteers all to be energetic and optimistic, respecting teachers, honoring truth, dedicated to the spread of Chinese traditional culture abroad, and eager to act as a bridge between the East and West. Soon we became great friends.

Over the last two years, they have organized various activities including translators' conferences, multilingual assemblies, cross-cultural forums, foreign language evening parties, and so forth. I have had the honor of being invited to almost every occasion. I feel very happy that I have not only found an opportunity to share my professional knowledge with them, but that I also find myself in a position to see how these young people move forward step by step, witnessing their achievements.

These young people all follow the teachings of their mutual mentor, the Ven. Master Xuecheng, whom they respect profoundly. I have had the honor of meeting Ven. Master Xuecheng in person on several occasions. His demeanor, dedication, charm and kindness attracted me when we first met. Ven. Master Xuecheng, his talents and his wish for sentient beings' freedom from suffering rather than personal goal of seeking his own comfort have influenced many people, including some highly educated intellectuals, to gradually turn to Buddhism. Many of them have chosen a path of spiritual improvement due to Ven. Master

序

　　2006 年，我就听说在北京西山凤凰岭有一座佛教寺庙叫龙泉寺，但一直没有机会去看看。2008 年，我的一个学生在那里做义工，他带我去参加了龙泉寺的中秋晚会，我很受感动。这一因缘让我结识了佛教和佛教界人士。

　　2009 年，我应龙泉寺翻译中心的邀请，开始为那里的志愿者讲授英语语言学课程。我发现他们是一群朝气蓬勃、尊师重道、乐于奉献的年轻人，他们致力于将中国传统文化弘传海外，架起一座沟通东西方文化的桥梁。我很快就和他们建立了友谊。

　　近两年，他们组织了译员交流会、多语种法会、多元文化论坛、外语晚会等活动，都热忱地邀我去参加。我很高兴有机会和他们分享我毕生所学的专业知识，同时，看到他们取得的一个个丰硕的成果，感到十分欣慰。

　　这群年轻人有一位共同的导师——学诚大和尚，他们都很尊敬和爱戴他，愿意听从他的教导。我有幸面见过几次学诚大和尚，甫见之下，便觉得他超凡脱尘，既有魄力，又有亲和力。在他"不为自己求安乐，但愿众生得离苦"的人格魅力感召下，一批又一批的社会人才，特别是一些青年才俊，渐渐加入到佛教中来。很多人因为见到学诚大和尚而选

Xuecheng. He has brought about great changes to many lives. With great enthusiasm, disciples engage themselves in the activities of learning and promoting Buddhism, giving to charity, helping to relieve disasters, and aiding the poor. These actions contribute to the harmony and stability of society.

Reading the Chinese and English publication of this book, *Stories of Ven. Master Xuecheng*, written by Ven. Huikong, one of his disciples, is a good opportunity for people throughout the world to better understand this great leader of Chinese Buddhist society. China is a country with precious cultural traditions. Every one of us should strive to inherit these traditions and carry them forward from generation to generation. Ven. Master Xuecheng has made significant contributions in this regard. He himself is a brilliant example and model for us all. He has been leading a talented group to carry traditional culture forward by using modern technology, organizing non-profit foundations to advocate and practice Buddhist charity, and encouraging international communication and cooperation amongst religious cultures. All of these achievements have enabled us to see the hope for the inheritance of the spiritual and cultural heritage of China.

There are few books in English on Buddhist culture, probably due to its profound and complex terminologies. While reading this English version, I appreciate the great effort made by the volunteer translators for their diligence and sincerity. I would like to wish them further success. May their ambition of translating Buddhist scriptures and traditional Chinese classics be fulfilled and their efforts prove to be fruitful.

Yang Chaoguang
School of International Studies
University of International Business and Economics
November 12th, 2011

择了心灵提升的道路；因为他的出现，很多人的生命发生了改变。他们积极热情地投入到学习佛法、弘扬佛法、做慈善事业和救灾扶贫等活动中，为社会和谐与稳定做出了很大贡献。

如今，这样一本由学诚大和尚的弟子慧空法师撰写、中英文对照的《学诚大和尚侧记》的出版，给中外人士提供了一个更多了解这位中国佛教界领袖人物的好机会。中国拥有宝贵的文化传统，如何将之传承下来并发扬光大，这是我们每个人都应该思考和努力的。学诚大和尚在这方面的贡献是卓越的。他本身就可谓"学为人师，诚为世范"，他还带动一批高素质的人才，运用现代科技弘扬传统文化，组织公益基金会，宣传和实践佛教慈善理念，积极开展国内外各种宗教文化的交流与合作……这些都让人看到了中国精神和文化传承的希望。

与佛教文化相关的英译本并不多见，主要原因可能是佛教教义的深邃和佛教用语的专业性。从这个译本的字里行间，我们能够看到志愿者们的探索和努力，感受到他们的用心和诚敬。衷心地祝福他们，在这条道路上越走越好，早日顺利地实现翻译佛教经典乃至中国传统文化典籍的理想！

杨潮光

对外经济贸易大学英语学院

2011 年 11 月 12 日

Preface from the Author

Thus is the Honorable Buddha: His wisdom is as vast as the whole space, knowing all without omission; his compassion and loving-kindness encompass all living beings, without any exception; his teachings on the wondrous Dharma extend through endless kalpas; his clear mind is free from illusions and reaching beyond language limits; his benevolence is demonstrated by examples of his embodiments; his sublime virtue is manifested in his awakening to the True Suchness.

The rise of the Great Way depends on development of a nation. Firstly introduced in the Han Dynasty, Chinese Buddhism experienced golden days in the Tang and the Song, was perpetuated in the Ming and the Qing, and declined in the early modern period. It is now on the path toward restoration revealing signs of prosperity. Nonetheless, the Eight Sects of Dharmata, Dharmalaksana, Tiantai, Avatamsaka, Chan, Pure-land, Vinaya and Tantra would usually hold on to their own doctrines, and Theravada, Tibetan and Han Buddhism would rarely exchange with each other. Alas, at such a declining age of Buddhism, even though possessing the aspiration as noble as the Buddha's to rectify the people's minds, benefit sentient beings and honor the country and all the world, how is it possible to have that fulfilled?

Blessed with virtue in childhood, Ven. Master Xuecheng, my esteemed teacher, started a monastic life at a young age. He respectfully followed the instructions of his mentors, vowing to inherit the Teachings of the Buddha as well as the ancient sages. In his twenties, driven by great compassion, he travelled near and far to take on the responsibilities of carrying forward the undertakings of the Buddha. Possessing the good qualities of a virtuous teacher, he integrates the three language families of Buddhism and bridges the eight Han Buddhist sects, mentoring outstanding monks. Accommodating the current conditions while keeping to the Unconditioned Dharma, he blazes the trail that leads to Buddhahood. He advocates for inter-faith harmony, regardless of their superficial differences. He comprehends all dharmas, despite of their variations in shape and nature. Auspiciousness is brought forth and evil signs are dispelled. Merits and wisdom are established and sufferings are eliminated. He enlightens beings with eruditeness in learning, glorifying Buddhism. He offers his deep resolve to serve all beings in the world, upholding the Dharma.

自 序

恭惟：佛者，尽虚空之广，智无所余；极众生之数，慈悲不舍。经劫浩荡，演妙法之辞章；幻念明澈，离言诠之乖违。仁心存乎应化，至德彰于真如。

所谓大道之兴，必仗国运。夫中国之佛教，始于汉庭，兴于唐宋，延于明清，衰于近世，昭苏于当今。繁荣之势，初露端倪。然，性相台贤，禅净律密，常持本宗；汉藏语系，南传上座，鲜有交汇。虽持佛本怀，意欲润世道人心以庄严国土，耀异域外邦以利乐有情，奈何教法零落，难酬其愿也。

恩师学诚和尚，幼秉玉质，少栖玄门，敬承师教，远绍如来，志万古圣贤；年及弱冠，驶大慈航，纵贯千里，近光遗法，担如来家业。现诸德相，融三系八宗，育法门龙象；无为而为，会时节因缘，开佛道通途。越有相之别，倡宗教之和睦；超形神之异，集百法于一心。云臻祥瑞，化天地之戾气；泽蕴福慧，济苍生之忧苦。以博学之明导化群灵，显扬圣教；以至诚之心深奉尘刹，住持正法。

A humble disciple as I am, I have followed the Venerable Master for almost ten years. As said in *Avatamsaka Sutra*, "Virtuous teachers, you originate the multitudes of all truths. Virtuous teachers, you generate the attaining of all virtues. Virtuous teachers, you are so hard to be met. Virtuous teachers, you are the source from which the jewels of knowledge of the ten powers are obtained. Virtuous teachers, you cause the vision of inexhaustible knowledge. Virtuous teachers, you cultivate the sprouts of goodness. Virtuous teachers, you reveal the door of omniscience. Virtuous teachers, you point out the way to enter the ocean of great knowledge." Remembering my teacher's infinite kindness, I ventured to take this opportunity to record some of his life stories.

Shi Huikong

At Yunshuitang Building, Putian Guanghua Monastery

In the Beginning of the Ninth Month, Lunar Year of Xin Mao

释子慧空，忝列师门，蒙慈垂教，几近十载。《华严经》云："善知识者，一切法云。善知识者，诸功德藏。善知识者，难可值遇。善知识者，十力宝因。善知识者，无尽智炬。善知识者，福德根芽。善知识者，一切智门。善知识者，智海导师。"随念深恩，无有穷际。故缘起之下，愧文才鄙陋，勉记片语云耳。

释慧空
岁次辛卯季秋之初
于莆田广化寺云水堂

目　录

CONTENTS

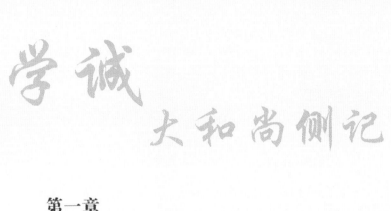

Chapter Five

Chapter Six

Chapter Seven

Chapter Eight

Chapter Nine

Afterword

■ 学诚法师常说：

"佛教的未来靠大家一起来承担，从我做起、从现在做起、从当下做起，因为利他才是生命的真正意义。"

■ Master Xuecheng often says,

"The future of Buddhism lies in everyone's effort. Start with oneself, start from now on and start from this moment, as benefiting others is the real meaning of life."

Chapter One

A Childhood of Virtue,
a Teenage of Determination

■ Master Xuecheng was filial and thoughtful since childhood. He spoke little but studied hard.

■ Influenced by his mother and grandmother, Master, at age 10, voluntarily became a vegetarian, and began to chant Buddhist scriptures at the age of 12.

■ Master showed enormous interest in Buddhist classics. He loved to read biographies of eminent monks, in particular, that of Ven. Master Xuanzang, a great master of the Tang Dynasty (618—907 AD). How Ven. Master Xuanzang pursued and spread Dharma, how his great vows were to "inherit the Buddha's Teachings, carry them forward, and spread them", all this exerted profound influence on Master's future determination to become a monk.

第一章

宿福深厚　少年立志

■　学诚法师自幼孝顺懂事，平日沉默寡言，学习勤勉。

■　在祖母和母亲的熏陶下，法师从 10 岁起就自发茹素，12 岁那一年开始读诵佛经。

■　法师很喜欢佛教典籍，对祖师大德的传记爱不释手，特别是唐朝玄奘大师的传记，其中大师求法、弘法的经历与"远绍如来，近光遗法"的弘愿对法师日后出家有着深远的影响。

Master Xuecheng, named Fu Ruilin, was born as the eldest of three sons on October 3rd (the nineteenth day of the eighth month of the lunar calendar), 1966, to a family of strong Buddhist culture in Luofeng village of Laidian Town, Xianyou County, Fujian Province. His grandmother was a Buddhist practitioner and later became a nun. His mother is a devoted Buddhist in addition. His father worked as an accountant and office clerk in the village. Being modest and courteous, his father is also known to be a benevolent man.

Master was filial and thoughtful since childhood. He spoke little but studied hard. He went to a primary school in Laidian Town, Xianyou County at the age of 8. In his spare time, he always volunteered to help his parents with housework such as cooking, washing, sweeping, fetching water, and plowing the field. On weekends, he would walk over five kilometers into the mountains where his parents collected firewood, and help them carry it home. Master's mother recalls, "My son would stay at home and cook when I worked in the field and attended the prayer-guiding services for the dying or deceased. On his way home from school, he often collected fallen leaves for the stove. Just think, he was only 9 years old at that time." Honest, tolerant and upright, he always behaved in a dignified manner, never looking around when he was walking. He never quarreled with other children.

Influenced by his mother and grandmother, Master, at age 10, voluntarily became a vegetarian, and began to chant Buddhist scriptures at the age of 12. In the evenings, he would chant and meditate until 9 p.m. before doing his homework for school. Therefore, sometimes he only slept for about two hours. Master's mother recalled, "When he was 15, I taught him to chant Shurangama Mantra. He learned fast and never had to ask me to repeat it more than three times. He began to cherish the idea of becoming a monk, but we, his parents, disagreed at that time, and he had to obey."

Master, from 1979 to 1982, attended the Overseas Chinese Middle School in Xianyou County where he was an honorable student. During his free time, he frequently visited the nearby Wangsheng Monastery (now called Jile Monastery). He felt a sense of affinity and familiarity whenever he was there. He especially liked the benevolent and peaceful countenance of the statues of Bodhisattvas. At that time in the village there lived a lay Buddhist named Fu Jinfu, who later became the Buddhist Master Ven. Dinglai and often brought Buddhist scriptures to Master. Master showed enormous interest in Buddhist

学诚法师，俗名傅瑞林。1966 年 10 月 3 日（农历丙午年八月十九）出生于福建省仙游县赖店镇罗峰村一个佛教氛围浓厚的家庭。祖母学佛并出家，母亲也是一位虔诚的佛教徒，父亲在村里担任会计、文书工作，是当地有名的善人，颇具温良恭俭让的风范。家中有三子，法师是长子。

法师自幼孝顺懂事，平日沉默寡言，学习勤勉。8 岁起就读于仙游赖店中心小学。读书之余，法师总是主动为父母分担家务——做饭、洗衣、扫地、挑水以及种田等。有时，父母在山上砍柴，法师就利用周末步行十几里的路程，到山上把柴挑回来。法师的母亲回忆说："我白天下地种田，晚上出门为往生者助念，他就在家帮着做饭。做饭用的柴火，有时就是他放学途中捡回来的落叶。那一年他 9 岁。"法师举止端严，走路时不左顾右盼；他品德端正、诚实，性格敦厚，不跟别的孩子吵架。

在祖母和母亲的熏陶下，法师从 10 岁起就自发茹素，12 岁那一年开始读诵佛经。晚上，他常常念佛、打坐到九点后才写作业，有时一天只睡两个多小时。法师母亲曾说："15 岁时，我教诵两遍《楞严咒》，他就学会了。当时他就想出家，我和他父亲不同意，他就不敢出家。"

1979 年至 1982 年，法师就读于仙游县华侨中学，成绩优异。学习之余，法师经常去离家不远的往生寺（现称极乐寺）游玩。每进寺院，总有熟悉、亲切之感，尤其喜欢寺里菩萨像慈祥自在的面容。当时，同村里有一位傅金富居士（后出家为定来法师）常常

classics. He loved to read biographies of eminent monks, in particular, that of Ven. Master Xuanzang, a great master of the Tang Dynasty (618—907 AD). How Ven. Master Xuanzang pursued and spread Dharma, how his great vows were to "inherit the Buddha's Teachings, carry them forward, and spread them", all this exerted profound influence on Master's future determination to become a monk.

▶ 福建仙游往生寺（现称极乐寺 上图现存老大殿 下图新建大雄宝殿和综合楼）
Wangsheng Monastery, Xianyou, Fujian (now called Jile Monastery). Above: the existing site of the old Buddha Hall. Below: the newly built Buddha Hall and Complex Building

带经书给法师看。法师很喜欢佛教典籍，对祖师大德的传记爱不释手，特别是唐朝玄奘大师的传记，其中大师求法、弘法的经历与"远绍如来，近光遗法"的弘愿对法师日后出家有着深远的影响。

▶ 2008 年 10 月 24 日 法师与母亲在北京龙泉寺德尘居
Master and his mother at Dechen Building, Beijing Longquan Monastery.
October 24th, 2008

Chapter Two

The Pursuit of Dharma,
a Period of Struggles and Rewards

■ Master Xuecheng studied even harder after coming to Beijing, modestly consulting others and learning from his mentors and classmates. He was so absorbed in thinking and reflection that he often forgot to eat and sleep.

■ In Beijing, Master always thought of his dearest teachers, Ven. Master Dinghai who lived abroad and was the one giving him ordination, and Ven. Master Yuanzhuo on whom he relied. Through correspondence, he reported to his teachers what he had gained through study.

■ Master was deeply influenced by the example of Ven. Master Yuanzhuo—his profound and compassionate vows, his patriotism to the nation and faithfulness to Buddhism, his modesty and calmness, his noble aspiration and unsullied behavior, and his self-restraint and lenience, all had laid a solid foundation for Master's future endeavors on benefiting the society and living beings.

第二章

求法时代　酸甜苦辣

■　在京求学期间，学诚法师更加勤奋好学，虚心求教于师友，时常因为思考问题而废寝忘食。

■　虽然身在北京，法师经常忆念着旅居海外的剃度恩师定海长老及依止师圆拙老和尚，常通过书信向师长们汇报学习心得。

■　法师耳濡目染了圆拙老和尚悲愿弘深、爱国爱教、谦默恬淡、志行高洁、严于律己、慈以待人的高风亮节，为日后济世利生打下了坚实的基础。

Master asked to take refuge in the Three Jewels (the Buddha, Dharma and Sangha) on the fifteenth day of the sixth month of the lunar calendar (July 16th), 1981. At that time, it was very popular at Master's village for the lay Buddhists to transmit the refuge among themselves. However, Master's mother did not agree with this and took him to a small temple on the nearby mountain where she asked the Bhikshu there to transmit the Refuge to Master.

On Chinese New Year's Day in 1982, Master went to Dongshan Monastery at Yuta village to pay homage to the Buddha with Fu Jinfu, then a lay Buddhist. Two days later, he returned home and asked for his parents' permission to become a monk. At that time, he was in his third year of middle school with only one semester left until graduation. His parents said, "Finish your middle school education and get the diploma first, then you can leave home." However, Master replied, "Why does a monk need a diploma? Let me be a monk, or I'll quit school. I'll stay at home to help with the farming and share your burden."

Master's mother took him to Dongshan Monastery to become a monk. There a lay Buddhist named Liang Jinliang, the later Ven. Chide, realized that the boy possessed profound, good virtues. He said, "You have plenty of virtues and should turn to a great Buddhist master instead." Therefore, Master's mother and Fu Jinfu brought him to Ven. Master Yuanzhuo at Putian Guanghua Monastery. [Ven. Master Yuanzhuo was a disciple of Ven. Master Yinguang and Ven. Master Hongyi, both eminent masters in modern China. Ven. Master Yuanzhuo once held office at Buddhist Association of China (BAC) as both Vice-Chairman and President of its Consultative Committee].

Master, led by the vows of his past lives, started his monastic life on the eighth day of the second month of the lunar calendar (March 3rd), 1982. The Monastery manager said, "A good day it is! Shakyamuni Buddha became a monk on the same day. You are sure to achieve full enlightenment in the future."

After starting his monastic life, Master was assigned by the Monastery to work on the farm to test his determination. Then, a week later, at the arrangement of Ven. Master Yuanzhuo, he practiced chanting Buddha's name in the Prayer Hall and learned to play Dharma instruments. He mastered the skills after three months, then he was eager to be ordained. At that time, matters relevant to ordination were decided by executive monks, while all Master cared about was to receive ordination as soon

1981 年农历六月十五，法师求受皈依。当时，当地盛行居士授皈依，法师的母亲不赞同这种做法，不肯让居士为自己的孩子授皈依，于是就带法师到附近山里的一座小庙，请寺里的比丘师父为法师传授了皈依。

1982 年农历正月初一，法师与傅金富居士去玉塔东山寺拜佛，正月初三回家后法师就跟父母商量着要出家。当时法师仅剩半学年就初中毕业了，于是父母就提出条件说："要把书念完，拿到毕业证书之后再出家。"法师说："出家人要毕业证书干什么？不让我出家，我就不读书了，在家孝敬你们，帮助种田，分担你们的辛苦。"

当时，法师的母亲就要带他在玉塔东山寺出家，那里有位梁金良居士（后出家为持德法师）觉得这孩子善根深厚，就说："你很有善根，应该去找大法师。"于是，法师被母亲及傅金富居士带到莆田广化寺拜见圆拙老和尚（近代高僧印光大师、弘一大师的弟子，生前担任中国佛教协会副会长及咨议委员会主席）。

1982 年农历二月初八，法师受宿生愿力牵引而出家。监院法师说："二月初八是释迦牟尼佛出家的日子，很好很好，今后必成正果。"

出家以后，寺里就安排法师下地种田，考验道心。一个星期后，圆拙老和尚安排法师去念佛堂念佛兼学法器。三个月后法器都学会了，就想剃度。当时剃度的事由寺里的执事法师决定，法师心想："不管谁剃度，能当和尚就行。"他给家里写信说："四月初八

▶ 1937 年 弘一大师
Ven. Master Hongyi. 1937

▶ 圆拙老和尚
Ven. Master Yuanzhuo

▶ 少年出家
Becoming a monk at an early age

▶ 法师与圆拙老和尚在福州法海寺
Master and Ven. Master Yuanzhuo at Fahai
Monastery, Fuzhou

▶ 1937 年 弘一大师去青岛弘律前留影（左四弘一大师 右五圆拙法师）
Ven. Master Hongyi before going to Qingdao to teach precepts (Ven. Master Hongyi fourth on the left, Master Yuanzhuo fifth on the right). 1937

▶ 2010 年 9 月 16 日 与定海长老在北京龙泉寺
Master and Ven. Master Dinghai at Beijing Longquan Monastery. September 16th, 2010

as possible rather than who would give ordination to him. His letter home read, "I will receive ordination on the eighth day of the fourth month of the lunar calendar." Master's father, worrying that his son would be too young to know how to practice correctly after ordination, sent the boy's grandmother and mother to Guanghua Monastery to talk the boy out of the idea, therefore, the ordination was postponed.

On the eighth day of the second month of the lunar calendar (March 22nd), 1983, as the situations permitted, under the arrangement of Ven. Master Yuanzhuo, Master received ordination from Ven. Master Dinghai at Guanghua Monastery. (Ven. Master Dinghai is now Vice-Chairman of the World Buddhist Sangha Council and President of Sangha Mahayana Indonesia.)

Shortly after the ordination ceremony, Master asked Ven. Master Yuanzhuo to teach him how to practice after becoming a monk. The Elder Master replied with a story, "During the Chinese New Year, the monasteries often observe a traditional custom of distributing oranges. Oranges are put into piles, with big and small ones mixed together. When your turn comes, you simply take one randomly. Why? If you purposefully take a larger one, you are greedy for profit; if you intentionally take a smaller one, you are seeking a good reputation, another form of greed. The story is very profound in meaning. There are people who act very politely to establish a good reputation; there are people who won't be taken advantage of. All of the trouble is caused by greed." Later, Master acknowledged, "I have been greatly inspired by this teaching. It reminds me to accept a situation as it is and act accordingly. The best option is to keep a natural state of mind. Confucianism also teaches that 'going too far is as bad as not going far enough'. Much of our learning and the way that we face various situations are generated from this awareness."

People went to sleep at 9 p.m., but the light in Master's room was usually still on after that. Ven. Master Yuanzhuo often had to knock at his door, urging him to go to bed lest the young man's eyesight be hurt due to exhaustion. Though so kind, the Elder Master was very strict. He required the young Master to learn classic works such as those of Confucianism by heart. Meals were not allowed until his work was done.

Once, when the young Master was mopping the floor in the dining hall, the Elder Master walked over quietly to find that the floor wasn't clean enough. The mentor immediately asked him to mop it again. When free, the young Master often volunteered to clean the hall and do dirty, difficult and laborious chores, which others didn't like to do. For some time, he served as a night watchman guarding Haihui Stupa (which preserves

要剃度。"接到信，父亲担心他年纪小，万一剃度以后不会修行怎么办，就让他祖母与母亲一起到广化寺劝阻法师剃度。于是剃度之事暂缓。

1983年农历二月初八，因缘成熟，法师在广化寺落发为僧。圆拙老和尚亲自安排剃度，礼定海长老（现任世界佛教僧伽会副会长、印度尼西亚大乘僧伽会会长）为剃度恩师。

刚剃度时，法师曾请教圆拙老和尚："出家怎么修行？"老和尚讲了一个故事："过年，丛林中有分橘子的习惯，当库头的把橘子称好，分成一堆一堆，里面有大的，也有小的。轮到你时，不要刻意去挑，为什么呢？你如果存心挑大的，那是你贪利；如果你存心挑小一点的，那是贪名，这是深哲理。有人客客气气，为得好名；有人任何时候不吃亏，是贪心在作怪。"后来，法师曾说："此话对我启发很大，一切随缘，平常心是道。儒家讲'过犹不及'，很多学问、境界都在这里面。"

晚上九点之后，大家都休息了，法师房里的灯通常都还亮着。圆拙老和尚怕他把眼睛累坏了，常敲门让法师熄灯睡觉。老和尚对法师的要求十分严格，给他规定了背诵儒家经典等课程，背不过就不许吃饭。

有一次法师在斋堂拖地时，老和尚悄悄地走过去检查，发现不够干净，就立刻让他又重复拖了几遍。在学习之余，法师经常主动

the ashes of the deceased monks and lay people) and the divine Longan Tree. At dawn, he would shift to playing Dharma instruments for the morning recitations. After that, he would serve breakfast to the Abbot and offer food to the hungry ghosts and Garuda through Buddhist rituals. He once recalled, "There was often a shortage of hands in the Monastery, so I joined the night watch. At first, I dreaded it a lot when patrolling around Haihui Stupa at night, especially when it rained. I also took part in construction work. It was a hard time. We had to carry the construction materials ourselves because there was no truck or crane available at that time. This was how my willpower and perseverance were strengthened."

Master was admitted to the preparatory class at Buddhist Academy of Fujian Province in 1983. During that period, he studied Buddhist scriptures and various other disciplines in earnest. As the monitor of the class, he was always ready to help his classmates solve various problems. He also took on the Monastery's affairs and supported the Buddhist cultivation and practice of the Monastery.

Master passed the entrance examination to Buddhist Academy of China in 1984 with honors and began his undergraduate studies in Beijing. He studied even harder, modestly consulting others and learning from his mentors and classmates. He was so absorbed in thinking and reflection that he often forgot to eat and sleep. One would never fail to find a dignified young monk in the classroom, always immersed in his studies, even on weekends or during holidays.

In Beijing, Master always thought of his dearest teachers, Ven. Master Dinghai who lived abroad and was the one giving him ordination, and Ven. Master Yuanzhuo on whom he relied. Through correspondence, he reported to his teachers what he had gained through study. In a letter to Ven. Master Yuanzhuo he wrote, "The atmosphere in the Academy is not suitable for study. Many students here are reluctant to study and practice, just drifting along day by day. It makes me sad to see this; I want to return to Guanghua Monastery." The Elder Master replied, "Do not mind what other people do. Just be modest and settle down to learn." The words greatly inspired him and kept motivating him ever since. In difficult times, these words enabled him to face his internal conflicts with courage, pray for blessings from the Three Jewels, overcome his difficulties and lift his spiritual level.

打扫殿堂卫生，做别人不愿意干的脏累粗活。有一段时间，法师每天晚上在海会塔守夜、看护龙眼树，第二天上早课时还要打法器，早斋过堂时还要做侍者出食。法师曾说："出家后，人手少，我就参与了晚上的巡逻和寺院建设工作。在海会塔巡逻时，常常会很怕，尤其是下雨天。那时很艰苦，建筑材料运不上来，要靠人力搬上来，毅力就培养出来了。"

1983 年，法师考入福建佛学院预科班。在佛学院求学期间，法师刻苦研习佛教经论及各科文化知识。同时担任班长的他，乐于帮助同学解决各种困难，还积极承担常住事务，护持大众修行。

1984 年，法师以优异的成绩考取设于北京的中国佛学院，就读本科班。在京求学期间，法师更加勤奋好学，虚心求教于师友，时常因为思考问题而废寝忘食。每逢周末或节假日，教室里总会有一位威仪具足的学僧在课桌前孜孜不倦地学习。

虽然身在北京，法师经常忆念着旅居海外的剃度恩师定海长老及依止师圆拙老和尚，常通过书信向师长们汇报学习心得。有一次他给圆拙老和尚写信说："学院较乱，大家不愿学修，浑浑噩噩地过日子，自己见了伤心，想回广化寺。"老和尚回信告诉他："别人是别人，你应当虚心学习。"这句话给他极大的启发，以至于在以后的日子里一直激励着他，使他在遇到困难时都能够勇于面对自我，至诚祈求三宝加被，突破困难，升华心灵。

▶ 在中国佛学院求学期间
Studying at Buddhist Academy of China

▶ 法师与赵朴初会长
Master standing with President Zhao Puchu

In 1986, Master was given an opportunity to study in Sri Lanka. When he asked Ven. Master Yuanzhuo for his opinion, the Elder Master did not agree to his going abroad. Years later, he recalled, "I could have acquired a PhD. However, I might not have had the opportunity to undertake the duties of the Buddha, working to help sentient beings as I have been doing now. It is crucial that one should always follow the guidance of his mentor." In his school days, Master also came under the special care and protection of Rev. Zhao Puchu, the respected then president of BAC. Rev. Zhao Puchu helped Master overcome difficulties and asked prominent and senior monks to guide him in his study and practice.

Master received a bachelor's degree with honors in 1988 at Buddhist Academy of China. After that, he furthered his studies as a postgraduate there. In December 1988, he received the Three Platforms of Complete Precepts from Ven. Master Kuanlin, the Abbot of Manjughosha Monastery of Chengdu in Sichuan Province.

In the winter of 1988, the Abbot of Guanghua Monastery, Ven. Yiran, resigned. In January 1989, under the care of Rev. Zhao Puchu and by Ven. Yiran's recommendation, all executives of the Monastery approved that Master Xuecheng, then still in the process of his

▶ 在中国佛学院求学期间（左学诚法师 右演莲法师）
Studying at Buddhist Academy of China (Master Xuecheng left, Ven. Yanlian right)

1986 年，法师遇到一个去斯里兰卡留学的因缘，向圆拙老和尚汇报，老和尚没有同意。多年后，法师回忆此事时说："如果当时留学，现在也许是博士了，但可能不会有如今承担教法的广大因缘。依师是重要一关呀！"德高望重的赵朴初先生（时任中国佛教协会会长）对法师也爱护有加，亲自请高僧大德指导法师修学，帮他解决困难。

1988 年，法师以优异的成绩毕业于中国佛学院，获得本科学历，并在中国佛学院继续研究生阶段的深造。同年 12 月在四川成都文殊院宽霖大和尚座下求受三坛大戒。

1988 年冬，广化寺方丈毅然法师退居。1989 年 1 月，在赵朴老的关怀下，经毅然法师举荐和全体执事通过，决定将尚在就读研

▶ 1988 年 12 月　在四川成都文殊院与清定上师
Standing with Ven. Master Qingding at Manjughosha
Monastery in Chengdu, Sichuan. December 1988

postgraduate studies, be appointed as Abbot of the Monastery. Master, deeming himself unqualified in virtue and capability to shoulder such a heavy responsibility, declined the appointment several times. In the Chinese New Year's Eve (February 5th, 1989), he left the Monastery without notice for Fahai Monastery in Fuzhou, preparing to return to Buddhist Academy of China. However, since he was still considered by all to be the most suitable candidate, Ven. Yiran, the retired Abbot, together with Ven. Yanlian, drove to Fahai Monastery and succeeded in persuading Master to return.

Thus on the eighth day of the second month of the lunar calendar (March 15th), 1989, an inauguration was held and Master Xuecheng, only 23 years old, took charge of the prominent monastery. He became the youngest abbot with the highest degree in education in a Han Buddhist monastery. During his term of office as Abbot, Master had been persevering in his studies. He defended his postgraduate dissertation successfully and obtained a master's degree in November 1991. After graduation, he

▶ 1988 年 12 月 在四川成都文殊院求受三坛大戒期间与三师合影
A group photo with the Three Acāryas when receiving the Three Platforms of Complete Precepts at Manjughosha Monastery in Chengdu, Sichuan Province. December 1988

究生课程的学诚法师推上广化寺住持的位置。法师认为自己的德才不堪担此重任而几度推托，并于除夕之夜（1989 年 2 月 5 日）不辞而别，独自去了福州法海寺，准备回中国佛学院。由于大家还是觉得法师是最合适的人选，老方丈毅然法师便亲自开车和演莲法师赶往法海寺将他劝说了回来。

1989 年农历二月初八举行升座典礼，年仅 23 岁的学诚法师成为全国汉传佛教寺院中年纪最轻、学历最高的名寺方丈。法师任方丈期间仍持之以恒地钻研学习，于 1991 年 11 月，顺利通过了中国

returned to Fujian, and was appointed as Vice President of Buddhist Academy of Fujian Province in December at the age of 25.

In November 1990, at a meeting attended by the departments directors of BAC, Rev. Zhao Puchu commented, "Remarkable achievements made at Guanghua Monastery are attributed to its former Abbot, Ven. Master Yuanzhuo whose efforts laid a solid foundation. The incumbent Abbot, Master Xuecheng, who is still doing his postgraduate studies at Buddhist Academy of China, assumed the position when he was only 23 years old. At that time, there were people who thought that he might be too young to take on the responsibility. But I said that it does not matter. During the period of the Anti-Japanese War, some of our commanders were only in their twenties. What's wrong with having a young abbot now?" Then Rev. Zhao spoke of Master Xuecheng again at Baima Monastery in April, 1992, "There is a young abbot in Fujian, who was a postgraduate student of Buddhist Academy of China. When he was recommended as a candidate for abbotship, some people said he was too young. Why shouldn't we trust young people? This Master Xuecheng has in fact done a very good job."

On November 25th (the tweny-sixth day of the tenth month of the lunar calendar), 1997, Ven. Master Yuanzhuo passed away peacefully at Putian Guanghua Monastery. Master's sorrow was beyond description. He erected a stupa for the Elder Master and wrote the inscription. Master had relied on Ven. Master Yuanzhuo for studying Buddhism for 15 years. Under the careful guidance of the Elder Master, he had recited and learned many Buddhist scriptures and Confucian classics. Meanwhile, he had participated in and witnessed the Buddhist endeavors carried by the Elder Master, such as reconstructing the Monastery, printing and circulating scriptures, establishing the Buddhist academy, and cultivating monastics. Consequently, Master was deeply influenced by the Elder's example—his profound and compassionate vows, his patriotism to the nation and faithfulness to Buddhism, his modesty and calmness, his noble aspiration and unsullied behavior, and his self-restraint and lenience, all had laid a solid foundation for Master's future endeavors on benefiting the society and living beings.

佛学院研究生论文答辩，获得硕士学位。毕业后法师回到福建，并于同年 12 月兼任福建佛学院副院长，时年 25 岁。

1990 年 11 月，赵朴老在中国佛教协会各部门负责人会议上说："广化寺搞得很出色，那是圆拙法师奠定的基础。现在的方丈学诚法师是中国佛学院的研究生，刚当方丈时才 23 岁，有些人认为他太年轻，我说，这有什么关系？抗战时我们一些二十几岁的年轻人就当了司令员，有什么不可以？" 1992 年 4 月在白马寺，赵朴老再次谈到法师时说："福建有位方丈，原是佛学院的研究生，推荐他当方丈时，有人说他太年轻了。为什么年轻人就不行呢？这个学诚法师就干得很好。"

1997 年 11 月 25 日（农历十月二十六），圆拙老和尚在莆田广化寺安详示寂。法师悲痛之情难于言表，亲自为老和尚建塔并撰写碑铭。法师依止老和尚修学佛法 15 年。在老和尚精心栽培下，他背诵、学习了许多佛教经论和儒家经典，还参与、目睹了老和尚建寺、印经、创办佛学院、培育僧才等佛教事业，耳濡目染了老和尚悲愿弘深、爱国爱教、谦默恬淡、志行高洁、严于律己、慈以待人的高风亮节，为日后济世利生打下了坚实的基础。

福建佛学院第五届预科班开学典礼全体师生合影留念 913

```
1 │
──┤ 4
2 │
──┤
3 │
```

▶ 1-3. 1989 年 3 月 15 日（农历二月初八）在莆田广化寺升座
Inaugurated as Abbot at Putian Guanghua Monastery. March 15th
(the eighth day of the second month of the lunar calendar), 1989

▶ 4. 1991 年 9 月 2 日　福建佛学院第五届预科班开学典礼全体师生
（一排左九妙湛老和尚　一排右八学诚法师）
Faculty and students at the opening ceremony of the 5th Preparatory
Class at Buddhist Academy of Fujian Province (Ven. Master Miaozhan
ninth on the left, first row; Master Xuecheng eighth on the right, first
row). September 2nd, 1991

Chapter Three

A Reliable Master across Many Fields

■ Master Xuecheng is very busy because he assumes dozens of different positions. Handling everything in an orderly and organized way, Master bases his methods on the principle of differentiating issues according to their nature, whether it is something general or particular, fundamental or non-fundamental, and in accordance with their importance and urgency. He works responsibly and efficiently, never wasting even a second. He considers dealing with complicated people, matters, and events as his solemn duty, not a burden.

■ Master is often heard saying, "One who is unattached does not fear; One who is selfless does not worry." He is always being amiable and kind, free and at ease like the drifting clouds and flowing water. He has never been disturbed by numerous affairs, whether in a quiet monastery or in a clamorous city.

第三章

身兼数职　认真负责

■　学诚法师身兼数职，工作繁重。他以"总别、本末、轻重、缓急"为处事原则，分秒必争，认真负责，视繁杂的人、事、物为庄严而非负担，每件事都处理得有条不紊。

■　法师常说："无我无畏，无私无忧。"无论是在宁静的寺院里，还是在丝竹乱耳的喧嚣闹市中，他总是和颜悦色、如行云流水般洒脱自在，不会因事务的繁忙而忧虑不安。

In October 1993, Master was elected Deputy Secretary-General of BAC. During his tenure, whenever he attended domestic conferences or paid visits abroad, he always modestly took care of the elder masters together with him. Through observation, he never failed to learn how to conduct himself properly, how to cultivate the mind through real life encounters and how to help living beings.

In December 1995, Master was appointed President of Buddhist Academy of Fujian Province.

In January 1998, Master became a member of the Standing Committee of the 8th Fujian Political Consultative Conference.

In October 1998, Master was elected President of the Fujian Buddhist Association and assumed the posts of Consultant for the journal of *Fujian Religion*, and Chief Editor of the journal of *Fujian Buddhism*.

On February 28th, 2001, during the 12th Session of the 9th Standing Committee of the Chinese People's Political Consultative Conference (CPPCC), Master was added as a member of CPPCC.

▶ 1993 年 3 月 6 日 与传印长老在一起
Standing with Ven. Master Chuanyin. March 6th, 1993

1993 年 10 月，法师被选为中国佛教协会副秘书长。在职期间，无论是在国内开会还是出访国外，他总是谦虚地承事同行的老法师们，从中观察他们是如何为人处世、历境练心、方便度生的。

1995 年 12 月，任福建佛学院院长。

1998 年 1 月，任福建省第八届政协常委。

1998 年 10 月，当选为福建省佛教协会会长，并担任《福建宗教》杂志顾问、《福建佛教》杂志主编。

2001 年 2 月 28 日，在全国政协第九届常务委员会第十二次会议上，法师被增补为全国政协委员。

▶ 2002 年 9 月 16 日　出席中国佛教协会第七届全国代表大会
Attending the 7th National Representatives Conference of BAC. September 16th, 2002

On September 16th, 2002, at the 7th National Representatives Conference of BAC, Master was elected as Vice President and Secretary-General of BAC, while holding the position of Chief Editor for the journal *the Voice of Dharma*. Master, then aged 36, was the youngest among the new leaders of the Association. For all this, Master responded, "I am grateful to those venerable masters for the trust they placed in me. I will devote myself to our goals and assist the President of the Association." Master has always lived up to his promises over the years.

On March 13th, 2003, Master was elected as a member of the 10th National Committee of CPPCC.

On January 16th, 2004, Master was appointed as Abbot of Famen Monastery in Fufeng County, Shaanxi Province.

On March 13th, 2004, Master took office as Deputy Secretary-General of the 2nd Session of China Committee on Religion and Peace.

On August 20th, 2004, Master assumed the position of Deputy Director of the Guiding Committee of Academic Titles of Tibetan Buddhism. He was the only monk in the committee from the Han ethnic group.

On April 11th, 2005, Master was appointed as Abbot of Longquan Monastery, Haidian District, Beijing.

In July 2005, Master was elected as a member of the Theory Research Council for China's United Front.

In September 2005, Master was elected as Vice President at the 2nd Session of the Youth Federation of the Central Government Departments and also became the honorary President of the Buddhist Association of Shaanxi Province.

On December 18th, 2006, Master was elected as Deputy Director at the 5th Session of the Chinese Association of Religious Studies. Upon assuming the position, he said, "We hope that people in academic communities and Buddhist circles will work together to create harmony in our society by fulfilling their own duties."

　　2002 年 9 月 16 日，在中国佛教协会第七届全国代表大会上，法师当选为中国佛教协会副会长兼秘书长，同时兼任《法音》杂志主编，时年 36 岁，是中国佛教协会新一届领导集体中最年轻的一位。谈起自己的当选，法师表示："这是前辈高僧大德对我的信任，我将尽心尽力地辅佐会长，并做好分内工作。"多年来，法师也确实在始终如一地实践着他的诺言。

　　2003 年 3 月 13 日，当选为第十届全国政协委员。

　　2004 年 1 月 16 日，荣膺陕西省扶风县法门寺住持。

　　2004 年 3 月 13 日，任第二届中国宗教界和平委员会副秘书长。

　　2004 年 8 月 20 日，任藏传佛教学衔工作指导委员会副主任，是其中唯一的汉族僧人。

　　2005 年 4 月 11 日，荣膺北京市海淀区龙泉寺住持。

　　2005 年 7 月，当选为中国统一战线理论研究会理事。

　　2005 年 9 月，当选为第二届中央国家机关青年联合会副主席及陕西省佛教协会名誉会长。

　　2006 年 12 月 18 日，当选为第五届中国宗教学会副会长。在任职会议上法师说："期待学术界和佛教界能够携起手来，各尽其责，共同为构建社会主义和谐社会进行不懈的努力！"

On January 8th, 2007, Master became Chief Vice President of Buddhist Academy of China and Director of the Museum of Buddhist Books and Cultural Heritage. When he assumed the position, Master solemnly pledged, "Buddhist Academy of China works to facilitate the future development of Buddhism, training monastics of high quality. It is fair to say that the rise and fall, the future and destiny of Buddhism in China rests, to a large degree, upon the development of Buddhist Academy of China. Being elected to this post, it is my sacred duty to make due contribution. I will assume this role although my ability is far from sufficient and I will take this responsibility as an opportunity to modestly learn from all of you."

On June 10th, 2007, Master was granted an Honorary PhD in Educational Administration from Mahachulalongkornrajavidyalaya University of Thailand.

On November 2nd, 2007, Master was elected as a member of the 4th Council of the United Nations Association of the People's Republic of China.

In December 2007, Master became President of Famen Monastery Buddhist Academy.

On January 13th, 2008, Master was elected as the First Deputy Director-General of the International Association of Buddhist Universities.

On March 13th, 2008, Master was elected as a member of the National Standing Committee at the 11th Session of CPPCC.

On April 10th, 2008, Master was elected as Vice President at the 3rd Session of the Youth Federation of the Central Government Departments.

On April 23rd, 2009, Master was elected as Vice President at the 8th Session of the Chinese People's Association for Peace and Disarmament.

On April 24th, 2009, Master was elected as Council member at the 10th Session of the Chinese Association for International Understanding.

On July 25th, 2009, Master was elected as Council member of China Social Assistance Foundation.

　　2007年1月8日，任中国佛学院第一副院长及佛教图书文物馆馆长。在任职会议上法师郑重地说："佛学院是我们佛教的希望工程、人才基地，这个人才基地不是一般的人才基地，是高级人才基地。可以说今后中国佛教的兴衰存亡、前途和命运有相当的成分是同中国佛学院有关的。让我来担任这个职务，虽然能力有限，各方面还非常地欠缺，但因为是分内的事情，我是义不容辞的。同时也是学习的一个机会，我很愿意虚心地向大家学习。"

　　2007年6月10日，被泰国朱拉隆功佛教大学授予教育行政学荣誉博士学位。

　　2007年11月2日，当选为中国联合国协会第四届理事会理事。

　　2007年12月，任法门寺佛学院院长。

　　2008年1月13日，当选为国际佛教大学协会第一副理事长。

　　2008年3月13日，当选为第十一届全国政协常务委员会委员。

　　2008年4月10日，当选为第三届中央国家机关青年联合会副主席。

　　2009年4月23日，当选为第八届中国人民争取和平与裁军协会副会长。

　　2009年4月24日，当选为第十届中国国际交流协会理事会理事。

　　2009年7月25日，当选为中华社会救助基金会理事。

On September 10th, 2009, Master was elected as Secretary-General of the 3rd Session of China Committee on Religion and Peace.

On September 24th, 2009, Master was elected as Council member of the 8th Session of China Council for the Promotion of Peaceful National Reunification.

On February 3rd, 2010, Master was elected as Vice President in Executive of BAC (to assist the president) at the 8th National Buddhist Representatives Conference.

On February 23rd, 2010, in Dacca, the Bangladesh Buddha Kristi Prochar Sangha granted Master the Atisha Dipankar & Visuddhananda Peace Gold Award for his remarkable contributions in the field of religion.

On July 17th, 2010, Master was invited to be Consultant of China Research Society for Urban Development and Consultant for the Medium and Small-Sized City Development Committee.

On August 26th, 2010, Master became Vice President of the 11th All-China Youth Federation.

On November 23rd, 2010, Master was elected Vice President of the 4th Session of the Youth Federation of the Central Government Departments.

On December 27th, 2010, Master was invited to be Vice President of the Institute for Advanced Study of the Humanities and Religion at Beijing Normal University.

On November 21st, 2011, Master received a Doctoral Degree of Tripitaka Mahapandit from the Sangha Council of All India Bhikshu Maha Sangha at Bodh Gaya, the sacred shrine where Buddha attained enlightenment.

Master is very busy because he assumes dozens of different positions. Handling everything in an orderly and organized way, Master bases his methods on the principle of differentiating issues according to their nature, whether it is something general or particular, fundamental or non-fundamental, and in accordance with their importance and urgency. He works responsibly and efficiently, never wasting even a second. He considers dealing with complicated people, matters, and events as his solemn duty, not a burden. He once said, "I give 30% of my concern to the present issues and 70% to things in the future. Therefore, the current affairs, having already been considered beforehand, do not need

2009 年 9 月 10 日，当选为第三届中国宗教界和平委员会秘书长。

2009 年 9 月 24 日，当选为第八届中国和平统一促进会理事。

2010 年 2 月 3 日，在中国佛教协会第八届全国代表大会上，当选为驻会副会长（协助会长工作）。

2010 年 2 月 23 日，法师在孟加拉国首都达卡被孟加拉国佛教复兴会授予阿底峡大师和平金奖，以表彰其在宗教领域所做出的杰出贡献。

2010 年 7 月 17 日，受聘为中国城市发展研究会、中小城市发展委员会顾问。

2010 年 8 月 26 日，当选为第十一届中华全国青年联合会副主席。

2010 年 11 月 23 日，当选为第四届中央国家机关青年联合会副主席。

2010 年 12 月 27 日，受聘为北京师范大学人文宗教高等研究院副院长。

2011 年 11 月 21 日，法师在佛陀成道圣地菩提伽耶，被全印度比丘僧伽会授予三藏大法师博士学位。

法师身兼数职，工作繁重。他以"总别、本末、轻重、缓急"为处事原则，分秒必争，认真负责，视繁杂的人、事、物为庄严而非负担，每件事都处理得有条不紊。他曾说："我平时用 30% 的心力考虑现在的事，70% 的心力考虑未来将要发生的事。今天的事我

too much attention; I must look ahead at the upcoming things while finishing up today's things. I never put off till tomorrow what should be done today. People tend to be lazy. Laziness has three expressions: reluctance to change by holding on to old habits, seeking excuses for shirking duties, and evading responsibilities. We should motivate ourselves and overcome laziness in ourselves."

Master told his attendant one November morning in 2005, when the sharira of Buddha's finger enshrined in Famen Monastery was escorted to Korea for worshipping, "Yesterday's meeting lasted until 1 o'clock this morning and after that I kept thinking about things. As head of the delegation, I am supposed to be clear-minded for things in all aspects. Those who are committed to shoulder the spread of Buddha's Teachings work around the clock."

Once, he worked overnight revising a speech, which was to be delivered at a conference to be held in Japan. He spent hours rewriting the speech over and over again.

Master once said with a smile, "I go back and forth between the BAC, Longquan Monastery, Guanghua Monastery and Famen Monastery." To promote Buddha's Teachings, one could hardly keep on without having strong will and great compassion. Master's example shows a sense of responsibility and mission.

Master is often heard saying, "One who is unattached does not fear; One who is selfless does not worry." He is always being amiable and kind, free and at ease like the drifting clouds and flowing water. He has never been disturbed by numerous affairs, whether in a quiet monastery or in a clamorous city. His mind dwells in precepts, concentration and wisdom, and therefore, is full of light, purity and happiness, a natural manifestation of his Bodhicitta. "It is just like the lotus flower shooting up from the water without getting wet, and the sun and the moon making their appearance in the blue void without being constrained by it." When asked how to cultivate this state of mind, Master replied, "Contain yourself; never vent your anger on others; never repeat a fault; reflect on yourself frequently; be considerate and try to put yourself in other's positions."

以前已经考虑过，所以不用花太多心思。要经常考虑将来的事，同时做好今天的事，今天的事尽量今天做完，不要拖。一般的人都会有懒惰的习性，懒惰有三种表现：因循、推托、逃避。要提策动机，克服懒惰。"

在 2005 年 11 月，法门寺佛指舍利赴韩国供奉活动期间的一个凌晨，法师对侍者说："昨晚开会到凌晨一点，之后一直在想事情。作为团长，各方面的事都要考虑得非常清楚。真正承担教法，是不分昼夜的。"

还有一次，法师为修改一篇去日本开会要用的发言稿，一夜没睡，共修改了十几遍。

法师曾笑着说："中佛协、龙泉寺、广化寺、法门寺，我来回走。"弘扬佛法，如果没有强大的悲心、愿力，是很难做下去的，这代表的是一种责任和使命。

他常说："无我无畏，无私无忧。"无论是在宁静的寺院里，还是在丝竹乱耳的喧嚣闹市中，他总是和颜悦色、如行云流水般洒脱自在，不会因事务的繁忙而忧虑不安。内心安住于戒定慧，便会充满光明、清凉、快乐，亦是内在菩提心的流露。"犹如莲花不着水，亦如日月不住空。"有人问这种境界是怎样修的，法师说："克制自己，不迁怒，不二过，常反省，代别人着想。"

Chapter Four

Integrating Learning with Practice,
Cultivating Virtue before Its Being Manifested

■ Since he took office at BAC, Master Xuecheng has been in charge of the nationwide promotion of normative transmission of precepts. He has been actively promoting in all Chinese monasteries the proper practice of chanting precepts every half a month and convening summer retreats. Master's endeavors have had a profound significance upon contemporary Buddhist history and will exert an immeasurable impact on the rejuvenation and spread of Buddhism.

■ Master once said, "I'm fully engaged every day. Without the blessings of the Three Jewels, I won't be able to manage. I am always in a position to take responsibilities when meeting with all kinds of people and things." Master preserves the Buddha's Teachings and perpetuates the wisdom of his disciples by dedicating his own life.

第四章

学修一体　内充外显

■ 学诚法师到中国佛教协会任职之后，主管推动全国各地的规范传戒工作，并积极努力推动全国范围内的半月如法诵戒及结夏安居。此举在当代佛教史中意义深远，对于佛法的重兴与弘传，将起到不可估量的作用。

■ 法师曾说："我天天忙，如果背后没有三宝加持的力量，肯定做不下去，面对种种人事，都要负责任。"法师是在用自己的生命延续佛法，延续弟子们的法身慧命。

It is said in *Ornament for the Mahayana Sutras*, a student should "Rely on a Mahayana teacher who is disciplined, serene and thoroughly pacified; who has good qualities surpassing those of the students; who is energetic; who has a wealth of scriptural knowledge; who possesses loving concern; who has a thorough knowledge of reality and skill in instructing disciples; and who has abandoned dispiritedness." Of these ten qualities, the six good qualities obtained for self-fulfillment are: precepts (being disciplined), concentration (being serene), wisdom (being thoroughly pacified), possessing the wealth of knowledge from studying many scriptures, possessing thorough knowledge of reality and having good qualities that surpass those of the students. The remaining qualities are the four good qualities for looking after others. They are: having skill in instruction, possessing loving concern, being energetic and abandoning dispiritedness. In the *Lamrim Chenmo*, it is said that a teacher is one "who instructs you in the stages on the paths of the three persons of different capacities and guides you to the Mahayana, which is the path to Buddhahood." Master often asks his disciples to integrate learning with practice and focus on cultivating virtue, letting it naturally manifest itself. Truly benefiting others and promoting Buddhism can only be achieved when one possesses virtues.

▶ 2010 年 12 月 在福建泉州承天寺传戒期间与羯磨阿阇黎 教授阿阇黎及十引礼合影
A group photo with Acārya of Duties, Acārya of Scriptures and Ten Precentors during the Precepts Transmitting Ritual at Chengtian Monastery, Quanzhou, Fujian. December, 2010

　　《大乘经庄严论》中说："知识调伏静近静，德增具勤教富饶，善达实性具巧说，悲体离厌应依止。"以上十种功德分为成熟自德六种：戒（调伏）、定（寂静）、慧（近寂静）、教富饶、达实性、德增上；及成熟利他德四种：善巧说、悲悯、具精勤、远离厌患。《菩提道次第广论》中说："此中所说知识，是于三士所有道中，能渐引导，次能导入大乘佛道。"法师常教诫弟子们"学修一体，内充外显"，只有自己具足了种种功德，才能真实地弘法利生。

▶ 2010 年 12 月 在福建泉州承天寺传授比丘戒
Transmitting Bhikshu Precepts at Chengtian Monastery, Quanzhou, Fujian. December, 2010

I. Precepts (Being Disciplined)

One feature of maintaining ethical disciplines is to subdue afflictions and obtain inner peace and serenity. One has to discipline his own mind before he can help others.

Master once recalled, "For years I spoke very little and quietly devoted myself to the Monastery before I became Abbot. As time passed, I became less distracted and my arrogance and conceit wore out." Every night, he kept himself engaged in introspection and reflected upon the few words he uttered in the daytime: which words were inappropriate and why? How could he improve his speaking the next day? Thanks to years of effort, his words rarely offend others. Therefore, other monks are willing to share their inner minds with Master and ask him for advice when they have a chance to consult him. They all like to get close to this compassionate "elder", which makes them feel at ease in his presence. He possesses the quality of natural affinity so that when people approach him, they imperceptibly grow on their way to spiritual maturity. When asked about the secret of this power, he replied, "Lower yourself, for all living beings are equal." Master lives a simple life, never choosing ostentation or extravagance. Whenever he goes out, he only brings with him a monk's yellow incense bag. He often says, "I come not to enjoy any material comfort, but to serve and protect Buddhist monasteries." His daily meals are simple and modest too. Master used to say, "Good food and good sleep destroy one's soul. Too much material comfort makes one forget his objective in life and lose his bearings."

Master holds many high positions and a great reputation, yet he remains modest and benevolent, never boasting about his virtue. He once went out in the company of a monk disciple. When they returned, the disciple wrote an essay in praise of Master's virtue.

一、戒（调伏）

戒的特质是破烦恼，得到内在的调伏与清凉。只有自己先调伏了，才能进一步去帮助别人。

法师曾说："我在做方丈之前，几年内都很少讲话，默默地为常住付出，久而久之，自己的散乱心、傲慢心、狂妄心等杂念都被磨掉了。"不仅白天很少讲话，每天晚上法师都坚持做自我反省，将白天所说的话重新回忆，反省哪句话讲错了，错在哪里，明天如何改善等等。由于长年累月的用功，法师讲话一般都不会损恼到对方。僧众与他交流心得时，也总愿意把心里话谈出来和法师分享，寻求指导。大家都很好乐亲近这位慈悲的"长者"，只要在他身边，就会觉得很舒服。他有一种亲和力和吸引力，使亲近他的人在潜移默化之中就能得到成长。有人问这是什么力量，法师说："把自己的身份放低——众生平等嘛！"生活上，他从不摆排场，外出时常常只背一个黄香袋。他常说："我不是来享受的，而是来护持道场的。"法师的日常饮食也很简单。他曾讲："吃得好，睡得好，一个人就没有灵魂了。物质享受多了，就忘失了宗旨目标，迷失了生命的方向。"

法师虽然身居高位，得到众多的赞誉，却一直谦下慈和，从不标榜自己的功德。一位僧众弟子在随侍法师外出后写了一篇心得，

Master read it and remarked, "In fact, I do not possess such great virtue. It is you who have the virtue, using me as an example to learn and understand Buddha's Teachings."

A netizen once slandered against Master on the website of Famen Monastery. Upon reading it, Master's attendant reported it to Master and brought it to him. Master glanced at it and put it aside, undisturbed. He said, "People have afflictions. This person is no exception. If what we are doing is good for our nation, for our people and for Buddhism, what is there to worry about?" When one maintains inner peace in the face of adversity, he is truly indifferent to fame and wealth, and has truly tamed the mind.

Master not only attaches importance to self-discipline and personal practice, but also initiates the spread and transmission of precepts. He once said in all sincerity, "The fact that precepts are neglected prevents Buddha's Teachings from spreading."

At Buddhist Academy of Fujian Province, Master used to give lectures on *The Four-Part Bhikshu Precepts*. In the monasteries he presides over, all monks have chanted precepts every half a month and hold summer retreats from the sixteenth day of the fourth month to the fifteenth day of the seventh month of the lunar calendar in compliance with the way set up by the Buddha (During this period, monks do not contact the outside world, settling down to study and practice). In recent years, Master has served many times as Preceptor Acārya, Acārya of Duties or Acārya of Scriptures in the Three Platforms of Complete Precepts Transmission Dharma Assemblies held all over the country. For instance, in March 2002, Master served as Acārya of Duties at the 16th Dharma Assembly for Transmitting Three Platforms of Complete Precepts held by the Buddhist Association of Fujian Province. In August 2007, Master served as Preceptor Acārya at the 19th Dharma Assembly for Transmitting Three Platforms of Complete Precepts, organized by Fujian Buddhist Association for Bhikshu at Pingxing Monastery, Mount Taimu, Fuding. In April 2009, when the Western Monastery of Hong Kong held its First Dharma Assembly for Transmitting Three Platforms of Complete Precepts, Master served as the Preceptor Acārya. In December 2010, when the 20th Dharma Assembly for Transmitting Three Platforms of Complete Precepts was held at Chengtian Monastery, Quanzhou, Master was again the Preceptor Acārya.

For years, Master has frequently transmitted Three Refuges, Five Precepts and Bodhisattva Precepts to lay people, guiding them well in their study and practice of Buddha's Teachings.

赞叹法师的功德，法师阅后说："其实我没有那么大的功德，你们把我当成一个境界，从中学习、体会佛法，是你们的功德。"

又有一次，一位网友在法门寺网站上诋毁法师，侍者发现后向法师报告，并将材料递给法师过目。法师只看了一下，便放在了一边，对侍者说："人总是有烦恼的。我们做的事情，于国、于民、于教都有利，还有什么可担心的呢？"内心面对逆境不为所动，才是真正的淡泊名利，才是真正的调伏。

法师不仅重视个人的行持，还积极倡导戒法的弘传。他曾语重心长地说："佛法不弘，原因是戒律废弛！"

在福建佛学院，法师曾亲自为学僧们讲授《四分律比丘戒》的课程。在他住持的道场里，僧众都依佛制每半月诵戒，并于每年农历四月十六日至七月十五日结夏安居。近年来，在全国各地传授三坛大戒的法会中，法师多次担任戒和尚、羯磨阿阇黎或教授阿阇黎。例如，2002 年 3 月，福建省佛教协会在福鼎太姥山平兴寺举办第十六次传授三坛大戒法会，法师担任羯磨阿阇黎。2007 年 8 月，福建省佛协在平兴寺举办第十九次传授三坛大戒法会，法师担任戒和尚。2009 年 4 月，香港西方寺自建寺以来第一次举办传授三坛大戒法会，法师也担任戒和尚。2010 年 12 月，福建省佛协在泉州承天寺举行第二十次传授三坛大戒法会，法师为戒和尚。

对于在家居士，法师多年来多次传授三皈、五戒、菩萨戒，善巧引导俗众学修佛法。

▶ 1995 年 9 月 27 日 在台湾南普陀寺拜访广化律师
Visiting Vinaya Master Guanghua at South Putuo Monastery in Taiwan. September 27th, 1995

Master has spared no pains to spread the teachings on precepts abroad. In 2005, he transmitted Mahayana Precepts to Indonesia, the first of such events in this country in 500 years.

It is noteworthy that Guanghua Monastery in Putian held a 108-day long Canonical Precepts Transmission Dharma Assembly in 1996. During this assembly, Master and many other venerable masters took an active part in promoting normative rituals of transmitting precepts in compliance with the way set up by the Buddha. This practice has already influenced the whole nation, including Hong Kong and Taiwan.

Ven. Master Daoxuan, founder of the Vinaya Sect of China, once stated, "Two (of the Three) Jewels, the Buddha and Buddha's Teachings, could not pass on and thrive without Sangha, and Sangha could not live on without precepts." Since he took office at BAC, Master has been in charge of the nationwide promotion of normative transmission of precepts. He has been actively promoting in all Chinese monasteries the proper practice of chanting precepts every half a month and convening summer retreats. Master's endeavors have had a profound significance upon contemporary Buddhist history and will exert an immeasurable impact on the rejuvenation and spread of Buddhism.

▶　2005 年 11 月　在印度尼西亚传授三坛大戒
Transmitting the Three Platforms of Complete Precepts in Indonesia. November 2005

　　法师还不辞辛劳地到国外广弘戒法，例如 2005 年将大乘戒法首次传到印度尼西亚，这是印度尼西亚 500 年来第一次传授大乘戒法。

　　特别值得一提的是，莆田广化寺于 1996 年举办了历时 108 天的规范传戒法会。在这次戒会中，法师及许多高僧大德积极推动以佛制规范传戒。这种风气已经影响到全国各地，包括香港、台湾等地区。

　　道宣律祖云："佛法二宝，赖僧弘传，僧宝住世，非戒不立。"法师到中国佛教协会任职之后，主管推动全国各地的规范传戒工作，并积极努力推动全国范围内的半月如法诵戒及结夏安居。此举在当代佛教史中意义深远，对于佛法的重兴与弘传，将起到不可估量的作用。

II. Concentration (Being Serene)

The scripture says, "Serene refers to having accomplished the training of meditative concentration. Meditative concentration is a mental state in which the mind remains peacefully withdrawn. This is achieved by relying on mindfulness and vigilance in one's ethical discipline, turning away from wrongdoing and engaging in good activities." Serenity is characterized by a peacefully withdrawn mind. Master observes that being serene refers to concentration. This concentration does not mean "being stagnant", but rather being very mindful of the external circumstances and our internal world. In this state, our mind is very alert and supple.

Once at Guanghua Monastery, Master convened an executive meeting. Each executive took turns speaking, reporting problems and voicing their opinions. After every executive had finished, Master gave a concluding speech that not only shared his own opinions but at the same time answered all the questions posed by them.

Despite his busy schedule, Master never forgets to study and contemplate on Buddhist scriptures. He has been heard saying, "I can settle down at any busy moment to read." Being able to maintain serenity whilst in motion is an indication of his Samadhi power. Once when he was abroad, he took several Buddhist books with him and read them during breaks at work. By reading during spare moments, Master could finish a thick book quickly, even marking essential points.

Master is a man of strong mindfulness. He once taught, "Our life is not counted by years or by days, not even by seconds, but rather by segments of thought. Our thoughts, one by one, whatever they are, make up our entire life. A day comes from the addition of

二、定（寂静）

经论中云："寂静者，如是于其妙行恶行，所有进止，由其依止念正知故，令心发起内寂静住，所有定学。"也就是对于所有妙行要进，恶行要止，用正念正知让自己内心安住于寂静，这是一种定学。其中说明定的特点是"内寂静住"。用法师的话说："定是内心的专注，但这种专注又不是一潭死水，而是对外境及内心十分敏感，内心是十分灵活的。"

有一次在广化寺，法师召集所有执事开会，大家轮流发言，反映问题，陈述各自的想法。各位执事都讲完后，法师总结开示，其中不仅阐发了自己的观点，还同时回答了每一位执事提出的问题。

法师法务繁忙，日理万机，却丝毫不放松对经论的闻思。法师曾说："在任何繁忙的时候，都能静下心来看书。"动中能静，这是定力的体现。一次出国，法师带了几本佛书，在工作空闲时就拿来阅读。只用空档时间，一本厚厚的书很快就看完了，并划出了很多要点。

法师的念知力极强，他在一次开示中说："人的生命不是用一年一年、一天一天、一秒一秒来计算的，而是用一念一念来计算的。我们一念一念想的是什么，加起来才是我们的生命，没有一念念，

thoughts. We should be clear about what to pursue and what to avoid in life. Otherwise we will not find clarity of our life's entirety. We must have command over our thoughts every present moment. If we lose command over thought this very moment, it will be mere talk to command our future." During his study at Buddhist Academy of China, he chanted the Great Compassion Mantra 100,000 times in three years. Disciples asked him, "How do you cultivate your mind while chanting mantra?" He answered, "Through concentration."

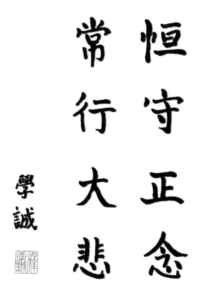

恒守正念
常行大悲
學誠

Ever keep right mindfulness
Always practice great compassion

Xuecheng

则一天天就无法计算起。我们的生命希求的是什么，远离的是什么，要很清楚。如果不晓得要怎么做，一生要怎样就会很渺茫，要从当下的一念去把握。若这一念把握不住，谈更远的不可能。"法师在中国佛学院读书时，曾用三年时间持诵了十万遍《大悲咒》。弟子们请益法师："您在持咒时是如何用功的？"他回答："培养专注。"

Glorify and succeed the lineage of the Unequaled Teacher
Maintain and perpetuate the wisdom of the World Honored One

Xuecheng
April 11th, 2009

III. Wisdom (Thoroughly Pacified)

According to the scripture, "'Thoroughly Pacified' refers to having accomplished the training of wisdom. This is done by specifically analyzing the meaning of reality in dependence on meditative serenity, wherein the mind becomes serviceable." Master suggests, "The root of Dharma lies in the ability to judge and choose. To have wisdom means to know how to choose between what to take and what to forsake."

Confronted with various problems, Master is always able to grasp the key points and make accurate judgments, which has gained him respect and admiration of others. The day before the opening of the First World Buddhist Forum, a person came with a question, "Do we have to wear Sanghati at tomorrow's opening ceremony?" It was difficult to reach an agreement about it. Master came in tactfully and replied, "It is better for us all to wear Sanghati. It will inspire people to develop faith. In imperial times, monks only used to wear Sanghati on having an audience with the emperor. Wearing Sanghati is very formal and honorable." The official in charge of organizing the forum thought that it made sense and announced on the spot, "All who will attend tomorrow's opening ceremony should wear Sanghati."

三、慧（近寂静）

经论中云："近寂静者，依心堪能奢摩他故，观择真义发起慧学"。用法师的话说："佛法的根本在于判断、抉择的能力，哪些是要的，哪些是不要的。知道取舍，就是慧。"

面对种种问题时，法师总能准确地做出判断，把握住关键，令大家心服口服。在首届世界佛教论坛开幕的前一天，有人问："明天开幕式是否搭衣？"大家一时定不下来。此时法师很善巧地回答："搭衣比较好，服装要统一，令见闻者生信。其实祖衣在过去是见皇帝时才穿的，很尊贵。"论坛的相关负责人听后觉得很有道理，当下就通知说："明天统一搭衣参加开幕式。"

IV. Having a Wealth of Scriptural Knowledge

Having a "Wealth of Scriptural Knowledge", according to the Buddhist scripture, "refers to being erudite concerning the three scriptural collections and the like." In a great master's words, "When the 'gurus of the Mahayana' give an explanation, they must enable their students to have a deep understanding. When they are putting the teachings into practice, they must demonstrate what is helpful at a time when the teaching is on the wane, and what is useful in the situation at hand." For instance, if a student has recently been finding others' faults, the teacher could use teachings to help eliminate the negative emotions of such a student.

Master attaches great importance to the learning and contemplation of Buddhist sutras, Vinaya texts and treatises. He always finds time in his tight schedule to do extensive reading on the Tripitaka. In particular, he has read many Buddhist scriptures over and over again, such as *Flower Adornment Sutra*, *The Wonderful Dharma Lotus Flower Sutra*, *Great Treasury Sutra*, *Nirvana Sutra*, *Mahaprajnaparamita Sutra*, *The Five Pure Land Sutras*, *The Sixth Patriarch's Platform Sutra*, *The Four-Part Vinaya*, *The Three Great Classics in the Nanshan Sect*, *The Treatise on Great Wisdom*, *The Treatise on Middle-Way*, *Maitreya's Five Treatises*, *The Treatise on the Illumination Door of the One Hundred Dharmas*, *Abhidharmakosa-sastra*, *Lamrim Chenmo*, *Lecture Notes on the Four-Part Bhikshu Precepts*, etc. Master has a penetrating and unique understanding of Vinaya, Pure Land Sect, Consciousness-Only Sect, Kosa, and Lamrim. He is skilled at drawing examples from one case to another and comprehending through analogy.

四、教富饶

经论中云："言教富者，谓于三藏等，成就多闻。"祖师亦云："言大乘尊重者，谓是须一，若讲说时，能令发生无量知解，若行持时，于后圣教，能成何益，当时能有何种义利。"大乘师长在讲说时，能让听的人内心产生很多的认知和理解，而且如果依照所听到的内容去行持，对于以后圣教能够产生利益，在听的当下也可以跟自己的生命结合在一起。比如说，某个闻法者最近观过的心比较重，师长的言教就能洗涤此人的负面情绪。

法师非常重视对经律论的闻思，总是在繁忙的事务之余，挤出时间广阅三藏，尤其是《华严经》《法华经》《大宝积经》《涅槃经》《大般若经》《净土五经》《六祖坛经》《四分律藏》《南山三大部》《大智度论》《中论》《慈氏五论》《大乘百法明门论》《俱舍论》《菩提道次第广论》《四分律比丘戒本讲义》等，更是反复研读。法师对戒律、净土、唯识、俱舍、道次第都有深刻和独到的研究与体会，能够举一反三、触类旁通。

Master holds the view that Buddhists should be tolerant towards other religions, willing to have dialogues and to exchange views with them. Besides his great dedication to Buddhist cultivation, he also reads scriptures from other religious texts such as the *Koran*. Moreover, he devotes a lot of time and energy to the learning of traditional Chinese cultural masterpieces such as *The Thirteen Confucian Classics* and *The Twenty-four Dynastic Histories*. He digests them thoroughly and is able to integrate them with Buddha's Teachings.

▶ 1995 年 9 月 27 日　在台湾拜访印顺导师
Visiting Ven. Master Yinshun in Taiwan. September 27th, 1995

Master not only reads many sutras and treatises, but also, for over a decade, wrote almost 100 essays of over 1 million characters such as "Enforcing the Soft Power of National Culture", "Religion Is a Hallmark of Human Progress from Obscuration to Civilization", "Let Us Share Religious Wisdom, Security and Peace", "Let Us Create a Harmonious World through Religious Wisdom", "A Harmonious World Begins with Our Minds", "Religious Concerns over Globalization", "Some Thoughts on Religions in China in the New Century", "The Past and the Future of Buddhism in Fujian", "A General Conversation about the Construction of Buddhist Talents", "A Brief Discussion

　　法师在勤修佛法之暇也研读《古兰经》等其他宗教的经典，他认为佛教应对其他宗教持包容、对话和交流的态度。对于中国传统文化著作，如《十三经》《二十四史》等，他也花了许多时间和精力钻研，并能够与佛法融会贯通。

▶ 2007 年 3 月 2 日　在北京龙泉寺德尘居丈室研阅经论
Reading a scripture at the Abbot Room of the Dechen Building, Beijing Longquan Monastery.
March 2nd, 2007

　　法师不仅广阅经论，十几年来，还撰写了 100 多万字的论文，如《加强国家文化软实力建设》《宗教是人类从蒙昧走向文明的重要标志》《共享宗教智慧　共享安全和平》《紧握宗教智慧　铸就和谐世界》《和谐世界　从心开始》《宗教关注全球化问题》《对新世纪中国宗教的一些思考》《福建佛教的过去与未来》《漫谈佛教人才建设》《略论中国佛教的文化建设》《现代丛林修学生活的趋势》《佛

on the Cultural Construction of Chinese Buddhism", "The Trend in the Life of Cultivation and Learning in Modern Monasteries", "Thoughts on the Secularization of Buddhism", "Buddhist View of Peace", "Crisis in Human Morality and Religious Concerns over Ethics", "The Role of Religion Should Be Brought into a Full Play in the Construction of a Harmonious Society", "The Building of a More Beautiful and Harmonious World with the Co-existence of Multiple Religions", to name a few. These essays have been published in domestic and overseas journals and papers, such as *People's Daily*, *Guangming Daily*, *Chinese People's Political Consultative Committee Newspaper*, *China's Nationality Paper*, *China's Religions*, *Buddhist Culture*, *Voice of Dharma*, *Fujian Religions*, *Asia Forum*, *Ta Kung Pao* (Hong Kong), *Wen Wei Po* (Hong Kong), etc. His works have also been published online at xinhuanet.com, people.com.cn, china.com.cn, chinanews.com, sina.com, sohu.com, fjnet.com, fjdh.com, etc. These articles have won popularity among many readers, both Buddhists and non-Buddhists. They not only reflect Master's understanding of Buddhist affairs, but also manifest his acute insight into state affairs and world harmony. Master has published dozens of articles in *Voice of Dharma*, journal of BAC, such as "Rely on Gurus and Listen to Buddha's Teachings in Learning and Practicing Buddhism Diligently", "Bear Purpose in Mind and then Establish Objective While Remembering Original Intentions and Wishes", "The Significance of Taking Refuge in the Three Jewels", "Hold Faith in the Principles of Karma while Practicing and Cultivating in Line with Buddhism", "Stay Away from Ignorance, Karma and Suffering, and Obtain Consummate Bliss", "Discipline Oneself with Precepts and Get Access to Bodhi", etc. Each essay, quoting extensively from a wide range of sources, explains profound ideas in simple language and yet with close reference to real life, integrating the teachings of relying on teachers and holding faith in karma with the teachings of *Lamrim Chenmo* about the Paths for people of Middle and Greater Capacities, so that learners can understand Buddhism from various perspectives and apply it to their lives.

教世俗化倾向的思考》《佛教的和平观》《人类道德危机与宗教伦理关怀》《应当充分发挥宗教在构建和谐社会中的作用》《让世界因多元宗教的存在而更加和谐更加美丽》等近百篇文章，发表在《人民日报》《光明日报》《人民政协报》《中国民族报》《中国宗教》《佛教文化》《法音》《福建宗教》《亚洲论坛》、香港《大公报》、香港《文汇报》等海内外多家报刊及新华网、人民网、中国网、中国新闻网、新浪网、搜狐网、佛教在线、佛教导航等网站上，受到教内外各界人士的广泛关注。这些论文不仅反映出法师对佛教内部事务的了解，也展现出他对国家大事及世界和谐问题的敏锐洞察力。法师在中国佛教协会会刊《法音》杂志上发表的各类文章几十篇：《依师闻法　精进学修》《明记宗旨　建立目标　不忘发心》《皈依三宝的意义》《深信业果　依法行持》《离惑业苦　得究竟乐》《以戒为师进趣菩提》等，每篇文章既能旁征博引，又深入浅出与现实结合，把亲近善知识、深信业果等法类，通达到《菩提道次第广论》中所讲的中士道和上士道的部分，让学人能够从多角度认知和理解佛法，又能与自己的生命结合在一起。

V. Knowledge of Reality

According to the scripture, "'Knowledge of Reality' refers to a special training in wisdom—the knowledge of non-essentiality of phenomena. In another way, it is said to be best if the teachers have a perception of reality." Master has studied Madhyamaka (the Middle Way) and Cittamatrin (Consciousness-Only) for years and has acquired a profound understanding of Prajna. He once said, "The Dependent Arising in Buddhism is characterized with harmony, namely, harmony among objects, harmony between human beings and objects, and harmony among human beings."

One morning after his daily practice, Master told his attendant, "I have been reading Buddhist sutras for five hours from last night to this morning, discovering the essence of wisdom embedded in the words. Words are more than words. Words in mundane books convey mundane dharma. Words in Buddhist scriptures convey Buddha Dharma. They are all made up of words, yet the meanings conveyed vary with the composition. If the essence of words could be grasped and used to understand our intrinsic nature, then wisdom would manifest itself and 'word Prajna' is attained. In this way, the mundane dharma is turned into Buddha Dharma."

The essence of Prajna is Emptiness. Emptiness and Dependent Arising are the two aspects of reality. Master is good at integrating the essence of Buddha's Teachings with what are currently acceptable to the public. Buddhism proclaims the Law of Dependent Arising. Therefore, Buddhism would keep in accord with the secular world, and help the living beings make progress from where they are. In view of this, Master often explains things in plain language. For instance, he says there are four barriers to upholding precepts, which are "material desire, family bond, fame and wealth, and wrong views." When practicing Buddhism, "one should not forget his ultimate goal, objectives, and original aspiration." Modern monks should possess five qualities, which are "aiming high,

五、达实性

经论中云："达实性者，是殊胜慧学，是谓通达法无我性，或以现证真实为正。"法师研究中观、唯识多年，对般若的内涵体会很深。他在一次开示中说："缘起法的特点就是和合：物与物和合、物与人和合、人与人和合。"

有一天早晨，法师用功后，同侍者随谈起自己的体会："昨晚与今早，连续读了五个小时的佛经，体会到文字般若的意涵。文字不单是文字，世间书籍的文字是世间法，佛教经典的文字是佛法，都是文字，组成的语句不同，其意义也就不同。能认清文字的意义，回归自性，成为般若，即文字般若。那么，世间法也成了佛法。"

般若讲的是空性，而缘起与性空是一体的两面。法师擅长将佛法的内涵融入大众眼前可以接受的缘起之中。佛法既然讲缘起，一定符顺这个世间，让众生从眼前这一步能走得上去。法师平时常讲一些朴实的话语，例如：持戒有四个关卡——"物欲、亲情、名利、邪见"；修学路上应"不忘宗旨、不忘目标、不忘发心"；现代出家众要具备"志、道、德、才、学"五种素质；丛林生活"坚持、随众、服从"是灵丹妙药；做执事，要"发大心、讲真话、办实事"；

choosing the right path, being virtuous, being versatile, and being knowledgeable." The best advice on the monastic life is "to persist, to accommodate oneself to others, and to comply." The executives of a monastery should "have noble aspiration, be honest, and do practical things." When dealing with people and doing things, the right attitude towards those who don't understand should be one of "acceptance, tolerance, courtesy and sincerity." "An incompetent person will not be able to cope with the ever-changing situations, so in the future, let those who cannot do things well do things, and let those who can do things well be detached from doing things." These words sound simple and plain, yet they contain the essential principles of Buddhism.

How Master associates with others shows his precise and accurate mastering of Dependent Arising. He knows the best thing to talk to different people, how to express and how to respond. For example, as to the reception of the Monastery, he once taught his disciples, "Whether to lead guests into the Reception Office or not, whether to serve tea or not, whether to invite them to meal or not, how many steps to keep from the guest while walking. All this have profound meanings." When in charge of the reception work for the First World Buddhist Forum, he received ten eminent monks within only one hour at the airport. He treated each one as an old friend, welcoming them with warm, genuine smiles. His deportment was very graceful. Due to scheduling conflicts, two distinguished guests had not been received. Master almost missed them but went all the way to catch up with them at the airport exit to express late greetings and sincerest welcome, which touched them greatly.

Prajna's unimpeded power (sovereign power of wisdom), which is not disturbed by external circumstances, is an expression of awareness of Emptiness. A disciple asked Master, "I've done a lot these days but somehow I feel depressed. What should I do to uplift my spirit?" Master replied, "When you finish doing something, leave it behind, do not be attached to it. Otherwise, you will feel quite exhausted. This is why I do so many things without feeling tired." Master always follows the changes of situations and is flexible in the means of handling things, which indicates his high level of cultivation. A story has it that Ven. Master Taixu, at age 56 then, once fell ill. A lay Buddhist paid a visit and advised him to give up all his concern. Ven. Master Taixu laughed and said, "Have I ever taken any up?" Every thought of Ven. Master Taixu dwelled in the Supreme Truth of All-Emptiness. He contributed significantly to the development of Buddhism and the well-being of living beings, yet he believed that all he did was simply in conformity with the arising conditions— all were like stage plays. Master also shows the same state of mind to some degree, just as a patriarch once said, "Being detached, I feel at ease at anytime but hard to tell why."

为人处事遇到对方不理解时，要"忍、包容、以礼相待、以诚相待"；"如果工作能力不够，就无法应付千变万化的缘起，以后不会做事的人去做事，会做事了应从中超脱出来"等等。这些听起来很朴实平常的话语，却蕴含着重要的佛法内涵。

法师对缘起把握的精准特别体现在待人方面。与不同人交往时，该说什么话，怎么说，如何应对，法师都极为善巧。如针对寺院的接待工作，法师教导弟子："来的客人，进不进客堂、要不要倒茶、留不留吃饭、走路时彼此隔几步，里面都有很深的用意。"在首届世界佛教论坛的机场接待工作中，法师在短短一小时之内，就接待了十位高僧大德。法师对每位大德，都如见故友，以真诚的笑容，热情欢迎，应对进退，不失礼节。因为时间冲突，有两位贵宾没有及时接到，险些错过，法师特意紧追二位至出港处，致以迟来的问候及最诚挚的欢迎，令对方非常感动。

内心不为外境所动的般若自在力，也是对于空性体悟的一种表现。一位僧众弟子曾经向法师请益："弟子这几天做了很多事，但不知为何心力有点莫名其妙地低沉，怎么办？"法师说："每做一件事，做完了你就要把它放下，不能再去执取它。如果你不能放掉这些事，一定会非常辛苦。我之所以能够做这么多事却不累，就是这样做的。"法师是时刻随顺因缘，方便办道，这是一种很高的修行境界。太虚大师在56岁患病时，一居士来探病，语大师"万缘放下"，大师笑谓："吾几曾提起！"大师念念安住在一切法空的胜义谛中，虽然为佛教、为众生广行利他事业，但是在他心中，只是随缘兴隆幻事。法师也略显如此境界，正如祖师云："随时皆得大自在，不能言其所以然。"

Facing praises and compliments from all, Master said modestly, "In fact, I did not do much. It is just that I gather and coordinate favorable conditions. Once favorable conditions are gathered, things will be achieved without extra effort."

▶ 2007 年 5 月 莆田南少林寺第一屆和諧之旅
The 1st Tour of Harmony, Putian Southern Shaolin Monastery. May 2007

　　面对各方的赞叹与嘉许，法师十分谦虚地说："其实我并没有做什么事，我所做的只是把各方面的善缘凝聚起来成办事情，善业一凝聚，事就成了。"

▶ 2007 年 10 月 莆田南少林寺第二届和谐之旅
The 2nd Tour of Harmony, Putian Southern Shaolin Monastery. October 2007

VI. Qualities that Surpass Those of the Students

The scripture says, "People degenerate if relying on those inferior to themselves; by relying on equals, they stay the same; by relying on those superior, they attain excellence; thus rely on those who are superior to yourself." The scripture also states, "Any intelligent person should not be distant from excellent beings and should rely on these virtuous beings in a disciplined manner. Once you are close to them, particles of their good qualities will stick to you." As such teachings say, students should rely on the teachers who have qualities that surpass their own and the key is that teachers should inspire great admiration and faith in disciples' minds so that the disciples could be convinced that it is possible to advance on the path to Buddhahood.

Once, Master took a business trip with a new attendant. On the evening before their return, Master asked the attendant to pack his baggage. Lacking experience, he did it very slowly and worse still, could not fit everything into the suitcase, which worried him a lot. At the sight of this, Master took everything out of the suitcase and rearranged it. He managed it without difficulty, neatly and with only one attempt, which filled the attendant with admiration.

Whenever Master goes out to attend Buddhist activities, there are always many Buddhists who want to get close to him. Master always tries to satisfy those who want to take a photo with him, beaming with smiles, never acting impatient, making sure that all devotees leave contentedly.

Inspired and attracted by Master's great personal charm, a growing body of outstanding people, young talented people in particular, joined the Buddhist groups. In the talent pool guided by Master, many disciples are well educated and have a Doctor's,

六、德增上

经论中云："诸人依劣当退失，依平等者平然住，依尊胜者获尊胜，故应亲近胜自者。""悉不应远诸善士，以调伏理修善行，由近彼故其德尘，虽不故染自然熏。"意思是说学人应当亲近德增上的善知识。德增上有一个重要内涵，就是让求学者在内心中对师长产生一种仰望，让学人知道这条路是可以走得上去的。

一次法师带新侍者外出，在返回的前一天晚上，法师让侍者收拾行李，侍者因为缺乏经验，做得很慢，并且最后有些东西装不下，让这位侍者很着急。法师见后，将箱子里的东西全部拿出来重新整合，很快装好了所有物品，整个过程干净利落、一气呵成，令侍者十分佩服。

法师外出参加法务活动时，总会有很多信众想来亲近。如果有人请求合影，法师都会尽量满其所愿，并始终笑容可掬、神采奕奕，没有丝毫不耐烦的情绪，直到信众开心满足地离开。

在法师特殊的人格魅力的感召下，一批批社会人才特别是青年才俊渐渐加入到佛教团体中来。在法师身边的"人才团队"中，有

Master's or Bachelor's degree. In *The Analects of Confucius: Book IX: Zi Han*, disciple Yan Yuan thus described his teacher, "The more you look up to his teaching, the higher you feel it is. The more you are engaged in the study of it, the more profound you find it is. Confucius is a good master, teacher and guide. He instructs me to read a wide range of classics and teaches me to discipline myself in line with decorum. Now I have been led to the right track and cannot help but make greater efforts." The disciples of Master have the same feeling toward their esteemed teacher. Many choose the path of mind cultivation because they meet Master. This is an indication of his surpassing qualities. Many people's lives have changed because of his influence.

▶ 2010 年 3 月 北京龙泉寺心文化之旅
The Culture of the Mind Journey of Beijing Longquan Monastery. March, 2010

很多僧俗弟子是在社会上就已经获得了博士、硕士或学士学位的高材生。在《论语·子罕第九》中，孔门弟子颜渊如是描述夫子："仰之弥高，钻之弥坚，瞻之在前，忽焉在后。夫子循循然善诱人。博我以文，约我以礼，欲罢不能。"法师身边的弟子们，也是如此仰慕法师。很多人因为见到法师而选择了心灵提升的道路。这是德增上的一种体现，因为他的出现，很多人的生命发生了改变。

▶ 2011 年 10 月 北京龙泉寺佛教文化活动
Buddhist Culture Activities of Beijing Longquan Monastery. October, 2011

VII. Skill in Instructing Disciples

According to the scripture, "'Skill in Instructing Disciples' refers to being both skilled in the process of leading disciples and adept at causing them to understand." Yet this skill does not mean being rhetorical. Instead it comes from the teacher's tender care and true concern for others, understanding for others' feelings and dedication to help them in the process.

Master is good at associating with people of various backgrounds. In conversations and interactions, he never fails to benefit others in the right way and at the right time. Once at a Dharma Assembly of Monastic Life Experiencing Camp, he talked with the camp members and answered their questions. He was so learned, refined, flexible, grave and humorous that the participants were thoroughly impressed. One camp member developed faith in Master right away and stayed behind at the Monastery, becoming a monk immediately after the Assembly.

On one occasion, a woman suffering from the last stages of cancer came to visit Master. Dreading death, she wanted to know how to face it. Master encouraged her in a relaxing way, "Death is nothing to be scared of. You have accumulated so many merits and virtues. This is a chance for you to go to heaven and enjoy your blessings." His words greatly relieved her anxiety and changed her state of mind. When something is said, its significance lies not in how well it is said, but whether it benefits others. A monk disciple, after hearing this story, remarked, "In my learning and practice of Buddha's Teachings, I only learn to be in line with the Teachings and do not know how to fit them within every situation I face. If asked the same question, I might have told the woman, 'Be mindful of death', 'Reflect on the fact that the three Evil Realms are nothing but sufferings', 'You

七、善巧说

经论中云："善巧说者，谓于如何引导次第而得善巧，能将法义巧便送入所化心中。"意思是说讲法者能够把佛法很善巧地送入所化者心中，但是这种善巧说不是一种能言善辩的技巧，而是在内心中真正关心他人，体会到对方的感受，并且在讲法过程中帮助对方。

法师善于与各层次的人交往。在讲话、应对中，总能契理契机地利益到对方。有一次，法师去参加"寺院生活体验营"法会中学员的心得交流活动，并回答问题。他的儒雅、灵活、庄重和幽默令学员们大开眼界，其中一位学员当场就对法师生起很大的信心，法会结束后就留下来出家了。

又有一次，一位癌症晚期患者来拜访法师，她对死亡充满了恐惧，于是问法师应如何面对这种心态。法师很轻松地鼓励她："死没什么好怕的，你做了这么多的功德，正好借此升天享福啊！"她听后心开意解，整个人的精神面貌为之一变。一句话，不在于讲得如何好，而在于是否能利益到别人。一位僧众弟子听到这个公案之后很是感慨："自己平时学佛法只知契理，不知如何契机，倘若来问自己，很可能回答'念死无常''三恶趣苦''忏悔、皈依、祈求'，但

have to repent, to seek refuge, and to pray'. The result would have been the opposite of my intention. My reply would only add to her psychological strain." With just one remark, Master took the burden off her mind. He was able to do this because he truly understood her feelings that he was able to benefit her, suiting his reply to her condition.

The preciousness of Buddhism lies in that the Teachings are relevant both to the truth and the specific conditions of people. In many cases, living beings are not difficult to teach, but the Teachings are given inappropriately due to lack of wisdom and compassion. Master thinks that to deliver living beings requires compassion, wisdom, and skills of all means. Compassion can move a person, wisdom helps one to choose among options, and a skillful teacher never fails to find approaches to a problem. Our theory will be mere words if we are not skillful in means to handle things, despite our compassion and knowledge of the Teachings. Compassion, wisdom and understanding people's conditions are indispensable to a successful guide. Imposing one's own criteria onto others closes the door for others. Teachings must relate well with people's conditions. Only through this method can Buddhism be spread. When socializing with visitors from all walks of life, Master always explores subjects in various fields with them. With his broad-mindedness, far-sighted thinking and deep cultural knowledge background, he almost never fails to get visitors to return productively.

Currently, many people, including some beginners in Buddhism, do not truly know what Buddhism is. Considering this phenomenon, Master has given a series of Dharma talks since the latter half of 2006 at the Dharma assemblies and intensive collective practices held at Beijing Longquan Monastery. The talks have been titled "Understanding Life", "A Life of Suffering and Happiness", "Knowing Life", "The Inner World: Lecture on the *Treatise on the Illumination Door of the One Hundred Dharmas*", "*Lamrim Chenmo: Vipashyana*", "Breakfast Talks", "The Path of Refuge", "The Path to Enlightenment", etc, and are released in print or on DVD.

Moreover, *Ven. Master Xuecheng's Blog: Essay Collections* (Vol. I—VII) were published in 2008. At the beginning of 2009, *Ven. Master Xuecheng's Blog: Message Collections* (Vol. I—VII) were published. The publishing of Master's blog continues. As of January 26th, 2012, 5 series (75 volumes in total) of blog collections have been published.

此时会适得其反，给对方更大的心理压力。"法师只一句话，便解除了她的心理负担。因为法师是真正体会到对方内心的感受，在她相应的那一点上去利益她。

佛法的珍贵在于契理契机。更多的时候，不是众生难调难化，而是说法者不契机，悲心、智慧不够。法师认为，度众生需要慈悲、智慧和善巧方便。慈悲让人感化，智慧能够抉择，善巧方便会有很多方法。如果有慈悲心、有佛法智慧，但缺乏对事的善巧方便，则只停在理上。若有慈悲、有佛法智慧，又知对方根机，依其机引导才好。否则以自己的一套要求人，则将人拒之门外，必须结合人的根性，法才弘得开。法师与社会各界人士相处时，常以其宽广的胸怀、高瞻远瞩的思想和深厚的文化底蕴，同来访者探讨各个领域的问题，几乎每次都让来访者满载而归。

针对目前社会大众乃至一些初学佛者普遍不知道什么是佛法、对佛教不了解的现象，从 2006 年下半年开始，法师在北京龙泉寺的法会及精进共修中作了一系列的主题开示，如《感悟人生》《苦乐人生》《认识人生》《心的世界——大乘百法明门论开示》《菩提道次第广论·毗婆舍那》《早斋开示》《皈依之路》《觉悟之道》等，并陆续制成 DVD 光碟或书籍出版。

此外，《和尚·博客》——学诚法师的博客文集系列之一至七册于 2008 年印行，留言系列之一至七册于 2009 年初印行。《和尚·博客》依次陆续出版，至 2012 年 1 月 26 日，已出版 5 个系列，共 75 册。

▶ "人生"系列开示光盘
Dharma talks on life, DVD series

These lectures and essays are simple but profound, providing very practical guidance for disciples to integrate Dharma into daily life. These essays were given attractive titles to be easily remembered by the readers. They include "Reflection on the Secular Pleasure and Buddhist Bliss", "The Significance of Building Up Ultimate Faith", "Seeking for a Life Instructor", "The Significance of the Wholeness of Life", "How to Get to Know the Symptoms of Inner Disease", "Correctly Discriminate States of Mind", "Break Self-centeredness", etc.

▶ 《和尚·博客》系列书籍
Ven. Master Xuecheng's Blog series

　　这些开示及文集深入浅出，很实在地指导信众如何把佛法融合到现实生活中。像"欲乐与法乐的省思""建立终极信仰的意义""寻找生命中的贵人""生命整体性的意义""怎样认识病相""正确辨析心相""突破个人中心主义"等标题，让人一看即能留下深刻的印象。

VIII. Possessing Loving Concern

The scripture claims, "'Possessing Loving Concern' refers to having a pure motivation for giving the teachings. That is, the teacher teaches with a motivation of love and compassion and does not look for gain, respect, and so on." His sole concern is to relieve living beings from agony and vexation.

Master once observed, "The most important thing in Mahayana is one's aspiration. We should use every thought to figure out how to benefit living beings and rid them of suffering." In a text message sent to one disciple, he said, "Whenever I think of the disciples who are inseparable from my life, I find no reason not to devote all I have. What do hardships matter? If I did not make endeavors, my life would be meaningless."

Master uses every opportunity to build favorable relationships with living beings and guide them on the path to Buddhahood. This is an example of his great compassion. When he goes to attend Buddhist activities, usually he has a fairly tight schedule. However, there is always a constant stream of people coming to pay respect to him or listen to his teachings from day to night. His attendant worries that such highly intensive receptions would be harmful to his health, but Master does not care at all. Occasionally Master shows signs of fatigue, yet he looks even better after talking with guests. He forgets his own fatigue while thinking of the suffering of living beings.

How Master teaches the disciples is their most unforgettable experience of cultivation. Once, Master was about to go out. Before departing, he asked his attendant some questions. The attendant, who happened to be vexed at that moment, gave quite confusing answers. "You did not answer my questions. You should be honest

八、悲悯

经论中云："悲悯者，谓宣说法等起清净，不顾利养及恭敬等，是由慈悲等起而说。"善知识在说法的时候，他的动机是清净的，不是为了名闻利养，而是为了解除众生的痛恼。

法师曾说："走大乘道，最重要的是发心，念念利益有情，解除有情的痛苦。"有一次，他在给一位弟子的短信中说："当我想起我身边还有好多不能分离的同学，我没有理由不为之付出我的一切，一点点辛苦又算得了什么。因为如果我不去努力，也就意味着我的生命没有价值了。"

法师利用一切机会与众生结善缘，接引他们走上成佛之路，这就是慈悲心的体现。法师外出参加法务活动时，行程通常都安排得非常紧，有时来求见法师的人从早到晚络绎不绝。侍者总担心法师的身体负荷不了这种高密度的接待工作，但他自己却全然不顾。偶尔法师会显出一些疲倦，但与访客谈完话之后，法师的精神却比之前更好，这是因为他缘念到众生的苦时，便会忘记自己的辛苦。

法师对弟子们的调教，是弟子们最难忘的"修行"。一次法师要外出，临行前问侍者一些事，侍者当时心里有些烦恼，回答得稀

with yourself!" reproached Master. Later, the attendant came to understand why Master reproached him. It might because he was older than many others, therefore, he would have few chances to be criticized and correct his negative habits thereupon.

► 2010 年 5 月 29 日　在北京龙泉寺见行堂举行安居仪式
Summer retreat ritual, Jianxing Hall, Beijing Longquan Monastery. May 29th, 2010

里糊涂。法师当下呵斥道："你没有回答我的问题，你要正视自己！"
后来侍者才明白，法师之所以呵斥自己，是因为觉得自己的年纪大
了，如果再没有什么机会被别人批评，就很难修改习性了。

▶ 2006 年 3 月 23 日 法师与弟子们
Master and his disciples. March 23rd, 2006

IX. Being Energetic

The scripture says, "'Being Energetic' refers to constant delight in others' welfare." A teacher should be resolute and determined when doing good for others.

In order to gather good karmas extensively and revitalize Buddhism, Master has, for many years, been working hard at rebuilding the learning and practicing system of Han Buddhism. He has proposed the idea of "Creating collective karma by working together on the Buddhist endeavors, and promoting Buddhist endeavors by relying on collective karma." Master is not only concerned for the monasteries that he presides over, but also for what course Chinese Buddhism and world Buddhism as a whole will follow. Such selfless resolution to work for the benefit of Buddhism and living beings is not just an empty slogan. It has been put into constant practice and can be seen through the growing number of Dharma assemblies, education programs for monks in Buddhist academies, and the work and duties assumed at BAC. Master is always at work without a moment's pause. He once said, "Now that I am in a certain position, I do things not on behalf of myself, but on behalf of the whole Buddhism and the fourfold assembly of disciples."

Despite being busy, he never neglects learning and practice, always acting as a good example. Together with other monks, he participates in morning and evening recitations in the Buddha Hall and eats at the refectory every day. He has been following such rituals for more than twenty years. He often says, "How could a monk not live a religious life? The head monk should take the lead for others and be a role model in learning and practice." Once in Famen Monastery, Master was preparing for a lecture and missed his meal. When he realized it, it was time to go to the Buddha Hall for recitation. The attendant intended to prepare some food, yet Master stopped him. "Food I can do without, but going to the Buddha Hall, that I must do." He said firmly.

九、具精勤

经论中云："具精勤者，谓于利他勇悍刚决。"是说在行利他事时，内心非常勇悍。

为了凝聚善业，重兴佛法，法师多年来一直致力于汉传佛教修学体系的建立，并提出了"以事业凝聚共业，靠共业推动事业"的思想。为了利益更多有情，法师想到的不只是他所住持的几所寺院，而是整个中国佛教乃至世界佛教的何去何从。这种为佛教、为众生的无我发心，不是空喊口号，而是被不断实践着：举办各种法会，佛学院僧才教育，以及在中国佛教协会所做的各项工作等，一刻不辍。法师曾说："到了一定位置，代表的就不是自己了，而是代表整个佛教，代表四众弟子。"

法师虽然公务繁忙，但从不中断个人修学，处处以身作则，每日随众上殿、过堂，二十多年来始终如一。法师常说："作为一个出家人不过宗教生活怎么可以呢？当头的要带头才能领众熏修。"有一次法师在法门寺因写一篇讲稿忘记了过堂，此时上殿时间已到，侍者要准备些吃的，被法师阻止了。他坚定地说："饭可以不吃，殿不能不上！"

Master very often rests for only two or three hours a day. When monks awake at midnight, they will quite often find the light still on in the Abbot's Room. In the morning, he gets up after hearing the beating of the board, which serves as the morning call. Sometimes he even gets up earlier. Then he sits in meditation. He also reflects on the Buddha's Teachings, takes refuge, makes Bodhi resolves and makes a plan for the day or does some reading. After that, he goes to the Buddha Hall for morning recitations and has breakfast together with his disciples. When the breakfast is over, he walks around and inspects the Monastery. Then he returns to the Abbot's Room for a one-hour meditation. In his early years, Master used to have summer and winter retreats for concentrated practice. Now he is tied up with many affairs and yet he still often manages to find some time for concentrated practice or a brief retreat. He once taught his disciples, "Our today is hard-earned and precious. We should not allow ourselves any slack. One fruitful day counts for more than a life in barrenness." Master's diligence encourages his disciples, acting as a voiceless reminder to fully use every moment and not to let oneself loose.

▶ 1989 年 1 月 在莆田广化寺大雄宝殿静坐
Meditating at the Buddha Hall of Putian Guanghua Monastery. January 1989

    法师一天的休息时间常常只有两三个小时。僧众半夜醒来，经常能看到丈室的灯还亮着。他早上闻板即起，也时常提前起来。晨起后静坐、思维、皈依发心、规划一天安排，有时也看书，然后随众上殿过堂。早斋后，他通常会在寺院四处走走看看，再回到寮房继续静坐思维一个小时左右。早年，每逢寒暑假，法师总要闭关专修，现在虽然事务繁忙，也会挤出时间专修或进行短期闭关。他曾对弟子教诫："能有今日，来之不易，不可丝毫懈怠，一天有价值比一生在空过有意义。"法师的精进行对大家也是一种策励和无声的提醒：要时刻把握当下，慎勿放逸。

▶ 2006 年 7 月 4 日　在病中仍耕耘不辍
Working in spite of illness. July 4th, 2006

X. Having Abandoned Dispiritedness

The scripture says, "'Having Abandoned Dispiritedness' refers to never being tired of giving an explanation again and again—to bearing the hardships of explaining."

Master's knowledge and moral integrity win the admiration of people from all walks of life. Whenever he goes out, many people become attracted to Master and want to stay close to him. He tries his best to satisfy their wishes. Once after a Dharma assembly, dozens of admiring disciples remained in the room and even the corridor was filled with devotees who wanted to see him. They all asked for Master's calligraphy as souvenirs. Master wrote over 30 pieces of Dharma words for the devotees, encouraging them not to neglect Buddhist practice. Seeing that Master was too tired, people did not have the heart to ask for more. Just when they were hesitating, Master asked, "Any more? All of you will get your wish realized today!" Afterwards, he told the attendant, "To cultivate good relationships and to have photos taken together with them are also Buddhist practice. We should be patient, compassionate, and considerate. Facing with situations, keep practicing the teaching on 'exchanging yourself with others'. If you put yourself in others' positions, what would you expect a master to do if you were the devotee?"

During Longquan Monastery's monastic summer retreat in 2006, Master had to go back and forth between downtown and suburbs every day. At 5 a.m., he set off from the Monastery for work in BAC. In the afternoon, he would be back at the Monastery around 5 p.m. From 6:30 p.m. to 8:30 p.m., he would lecture on Bhikshu precepts for monks. When class was over, though exhausted, he would satisfy the monk disciples who eagerly followed him into the Abbot's Room to ask questions. Sometimes, the disciples would not leave until late after bedtime, or even midnight. It was then that Master had time to take up other business and begin his own routine practice.

十、远离厌患

如经论中云："远离厌患者，数数宣说而无疲倦，谓能堪忍宣说苦劳。"

法师的学问人品，受到社会各界人士的敬仰。每次外出，都会有很多人想亲近法师，法师也总是尽可能地满众生的愿。有一次法会结束后，客厅里聚集了数十位仰慕法师的弟子，整个走廊里也站满了要见法师的信徒，大家纷纷请求法师题字留念。法师连续写了三十余幅法语同信众结缘并勉励大家勿忘修行。大家看到法师太累了，都不忍心再上前求字，正在踌躇之间，法师却主动问："大家还有要写的吗？今天都一一满愿！"事后，法师对侍者说："和信众结缘、照相都是修行，要有耐心、慈心、悲心，对境界多作'自他相换'之想，假如你是信徒，你会期待别人怎样做呢？"

2006 年龙泉寺僧众结夏安居期间，法师每天往返于京城与京郊，早晨五点多从寺院出发去中国佛教协会办公，下午五点左右再返回寺内，晚上六点半至八点半为僧众讲比丘戒。下课之后，法师虽然已经很累了，但若看到仍有弟子怀着强烈的希求心到丈室请益，法师也都一一满足大家。有时迟至晚上十点半甚至零点之后，弟子们才依依不舍地离去，而法师随后还要处理公务及自修用功。

Master once said, "I'm fully engaged every day. Without the blessings of the Three Jewels, I won't be able to manage. I am always in a position to take responsibilities when meeting with all kinds of people and things." Master preserves the Buddha's Teachings and perpetuates the wisdom of his disciples by dedicating his own life. "He never grows weary of learning or becomes impatient when teaching." "He forgets his food in his eager pursuit of knowledge; he forgets his sorrows in the joy of its attainment, and he does not perceive that old age is coming on."

Being able to integrate learning with practice and cultivate virtue before its being manifested, in his disciples' minds, Master is such a true teacher. He has taken the lead and sets good examples for Buddhist practice, upholding and protecting Buddha's Teachings. He has achieved affirmative appreciation from Rev. Zhao Puchu who once remarked on Master in a poem. "He is strict with himself, yet he handles things gently. Though he studies and practices within the Monastery, his teachings are spread far and wide. How does one establish a place for Buddhist practice? One may find the answer in his example." Such is the sincere approval and ardent expectation of a young monk, given by a prestigious elder, a century figure.

他曾说："我天天忙，如果背后没有三宝加持的力量，肯定做不下去，面对种种人事，都要负责任。"法师是在用自己的生命延续佛法，延续弟子们的法身慧命。"学而不厌，诲人不倦。""发愤忘食，乐以忘忧，不知老之将至云尔。"

"学修一体，内充外显"，在弟子们心中，法师是这样一位善知识。法师领众修学、住持正法的高风懿行，更是得到赵朴老的肯定与赞叹。朴老曾为法师题诗曰："律己其志刚，接物其气柔；学修不出门，声教及遐陬；如何办道场，傥于此间求。"这是一位世纪老人对一个青年晚辈的嘉许，更是一种殷殷的期望。

Chapter Five

Building Monasteries and Academies, Nurturing Outstanding Buddhists

■ Under the continuous exploration of Master Xuecheng, Longquan Monastery has inherited the best of the traditional monastic system while absorbing the characteristics of modern institutional Buddhist education. Therefore a high quality Sangha has come into shape.

■ Master advocates integrating three language families of Buddhism and promoting all eight sects of Han Buddhism. With such a vision, Master has brought forward and implemented the idea of Four Becomings: "the monastery becoming academic, the academy becoming monastic, the learning and practice becoming integrated, and the management becoming scientific."

第五章

两院建设 培育英才

■ 在学诚法师的不断总结摸索下，龙泉寺僧团既继承了
传统丛林的精华，又汲取了现代佛学院教育的特点，形
成了高素质的僧团。

■ 法师以三大语系并融、八大宗派并弘的胸怀，前瞻性
地提出并实践"丛林学院化，学院丛林化，修学一体化，
管理科学化"的"四化"办学理念。

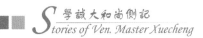

I. Presiding over Monasteries

i. Putian Guanghua Monastery

一、住持寺院

1. 莆田广化寺

Putian Guanghua Monastery is one of the major monasteries in Fujian Province. As the Abbot of Guanghua Monastery, Master has been conscientiously working at the infrastructural construction of the Monastery, organizational planning, personnel arrangement, management system, education and life of the Monastery, and quality improvement of individuals and the community as well. Under Master's leadership, the number of residents of Guanghua Monastery has increased from around 100 to over 260. For years, Guanghua Monastery has insisted on the "Three Don'ts": "Do not charge admissions, do not set up commercial shops and do not perform commercialized Buddhist services." The religious community commits itself to teaching all living beings as well as promoting a harmonious society. Guanghua Monastery offers, with an average living condition, relatively low allowances among monasteries of its kind all over the nation. Providing such an environment, the Monastery has cultivated teams of outstanding monks who have firm resolve, pure faith, high moral attainments and are willing to live a simple and virtuous life. Guanghua Monastery is regarded as one of the best examples of Buddhist societies for its strict adherence to traditional Buddhist precepts and its emphasis on Buddhist culture and education. President Zhao Puchu, eulogized Guanghua Monastery as one of the three model monasteries in China.

▶ 1990 年 10 月 迎接赵朴初会长视察莆田广化寺
Receiving President Zhao Puchu at Putian Guanghua Monastery. October 1990

　　福建莆田广化寺是八闽佛教一大丛林。从寺院建设到组织规划、从人事安排到管理制度、从寺院教育到丛林生活、从自身修养的提高到整体素质的加强，法师样样操劳，尽职尽责。在他的住持领导下，住众由原来的100人左右增加至260多人。多年来，广化寺始终坚持"不卖门票，不设商业网点，不赶经忏"的"三不"原则，把寺院的职能真正落实到教化众生、和谐社会上去。住众单资是全国同类丛林中较少的，生活条件也是一般水平，在这样的环境下，寺院培养出了一批批道心坚固、信仰纯正、德行高洁、安贫乐道的法门龙象，并以坚守佛教传统戒律和重视佛教文化教育事业两方面的成绩被佛教界立为榜样，被赵朴初会长誉为全国三大模范丛林之一。

▶ 1990 年 10 月 在莆田广化寺（左二妙湛老和尚 左三学诚法师 中间赵朴初会长）
At Putian Guanghua Monastery (Ven. Master Miaozhan second on the left, Master Xuecheng third on the left, President Zhao Puchu in the middle). October 1990

In November 1990, President Zhao Puchu made an inspection tour to a monastery and said, "Guanghua Monastery, led by Master Xuecheng, attaches great importance to Buddhist practice. They handle things in accordance with Buddhist principles and never yield to the way of the secular world. They've done a good job of it. I made offerings to the Sangha with vegetarian meals and have had lunch there with others. I was deeply moved by their religious lifestyle, strictly in accordance with the Teachings and the Vinaya. Their wall posters, preaching about Buddhism while also promoting secular ethics helped both monks and people outside monasteries understand each other. The effects are very good." Just as what he used to describe, "Upon entering the Monastery, the determination of cultivation grows and the tradition of South Mount (Guanghua Monastery) is kept. Dignified manner and perfect order are manifested in the dining hall. The benevolence of living beings is reflected upon, even when a grain of rice is consumed."

Every time Master returns to Guanghua Monastery, even if he doesn't arrive until midnight, he would attend morning recitations with the Sangha on the following day. Master often asks the executive monks to update the situations of the Monastery. He has a special concern for the watchmen and often walks around at the Monastery between 10 p.m. to 11 p.m. to talk with them.

▶ 1990 年 10 月 与赵朴初会长在莆田广化寺大雄宝殿
Master with President Zhao Puchu at the Buddha Hall of Putian Guanghua Monastery. October, 1990

　　1990 年 11 月，赵朴初会长在视察寺院时说："学诚法师住持的广化寺，着重在道行，根据佛教原则办事，决不迁就人情。这一点，坚持得好。我在广化寺供了斋，也随众过了堂，看到他们如法如律的宗教生活，我深受感动。他们办的壁报，一方面宣讲佛法，一方面宣传在社会上做人的道德，不但让寺庙里的人了解社会，也让社会上的人了解僧人，效果很好。"正所谓："一入山门长道心，南山风范见传承。威仪秩序斋堂里，粒米当思大众恩。"

　　法师每次回广化寺，哪怕是半夜，次日也都要和大众一起上早课。他经常找执事法师了解寺院的情况，还特别关心巡夜人员，常常会于晚上十点到十一点左右在寺院走走，和他们谈话。

▶ 2003 年 10 月 1 日 在莆田广化寺早课上
At the morning recitation of Putian Guanghua Monastery. October 1st, 2003

He is amiable and easy-going, never pretentious. Master cares for every member of the Sangha, from the elders to the novices. He is strict with himself and lenient towards others. When monks encounter problems, Master's guidance is so tactful that they always accept his teachings happily.

Master often says, "In order to rectify the current abuses of transmitting precepts, accepting disciples, performing commercialized Buddhist rituals and accommodating travelling monks in an indiscriminate way, we must emphasize, study and promote precepts." From October 1996 to January 1997, Buddhist Association of China and Putian Guanghua Monastery jointly organized an unprecedented 108-day Canonical Precepts Transmission Dharma Assembly. At the working meeting of BAC in April 1997, Rev. Zhao Puchu spoke highly of this event, "Some work has been done in recent years. For instance, Master Xuecheng's holding the Canonical Precepts Transmission at Putian Guanghua Monastery received positive public response."

In April 2003, Guanghua Monastery held another Dharma Assembly for Transmitting the Three Platforms of Complete Precepts, which complied with the Teachings and the Vinaya. 340 monks from 25 regions of China and such countries as Singapore, Malaysia attended the precepts transmission. As the Preceptor Acārya for precepts transmission, Master was very concerned about the operation of the Assembly. He chaired the planning of the Assembly, attended the precentors' conclusion meetings every night and gave instructions on everything from the overall pace of the Dharma Assembly to the details, and he also made timely adjustments according to the situation. Master held great expectations for the preceptees, instructing them as monks to establish right views, cherish the great opportunity of the Assembly and sincerely repent and vow so as to gain the pure substance of precepts. At the same time, the preceptees should make a vast and great resolve to devote all they have to the revitalization of Buddhism.

In order to provide the resident monastics with more opportunities of learning and contemplating Buddhist scriptures, Master set up Dharma study classes for the monastic community. The curriculum mainly covers recitation of Mahayana sutras such as *Mahaprajnaparamita Sutra*, *The Wonderful Dharma Lotus Flower Sutra*, and study of *Lamrim Chenmo*, *Outline of Nanshan Precepts for Laity*, *Manual for Buddhist Novice*, *The Four-Part Bhikshu Precepts*, etc. The courses have greatly helped the monastics with their scriptural study, who had been overwhelmingly occupied with work and various

　　法师平易近人，从不摆架子，上到老和尚下到小沙弥，他对寺里的每一位僧众都非常关心。法师严于律己，宽以待人，对僧众的问题会委婉善巧地开导，令对方心悦诚服，欢喜领受。

　　法师常说："要想改善目前佛教界滥传戒、滥收徒、滥赶经忏、滥挂单的现象，必须重视戒律、学习戒律、弘扬戒律。"1996 年 10 月至 1997 年 1 月，中国佛教协会与莆田广化寺联合举办了 108 天盛况空前的规范传戒法会。在 1997 年 4 月的中国佛教协会办公会议上，赵朴老对此给予了赞叹："这几年我们做了一些工作，如学诚法师在莆田广化寺搞的规范传戒，舆论反应很好。"

　　2003 年 4 月，广化寺再次如法如律地举办了传授三坛大戒的法会，来自全国 25 个地区和新加坡、马来西亚的 340 名僧众参加了受戒。作为戒和尚的学诚法师，十分关心戒会的运作情况，亲自主持制定规划并参加每天晚上的引礼结行会，现场给予指导，从整体到细节上把握法会的节奏，并随顺因缘及时作出调整。法师对戒子们寄予厚望，他教导戒子们应树立起出家修行的正知见，要珍视戒会的殊胜因缘，殷重忏悔发愿，以期得到清净圆满的戒体，同时当发广大心，为振兴佛教而奉献自己的一切。

　　为使常住僧众也能多闻思经论，法师在常住开设了佛法学习班，主要读诵《大般若经》《法华经》等大乘经典，学习《菩提道次第广论》《南山律在家备览》《沙弥律仪》《四分律比丘戒》等，弥补了长期以来寺院僧众以承担做事为主而缺乏闻思的不足。他多次告诫大家，无论在社会上还是佛教内部，教育的核心作用是不可

chores. Master told his disciples for many times that the core role of education could not be changed, either in the secular world or in the Buddhist circle. The older that people get, the harder they can change their habits. Therefore, cultivation should start from the youth so as to promote the development of Buddhism in different places. Monks come from lay people. Only when lay people are equipped with the right views to practice in accordance with the Buddha's Teachings and become monastics, can such a Sangha truly protect and uphold the Dharma, promote the Buddha's Teachings, benefit living beings, glorify and succeed the lineage of the Unequaled Teacher, maintain and perpetuate the wisdom of the World Honored One. Influenced by Master's thoughts and charm in personality, more and more outstanding people, especially young intellectuals, come to join the Sangha.

▶ 2003 年 4 月 在莆田广化寺传授三坛大戒
Transmitting the Three Platforms of Complete Precepts at Putian Guanghua Monastery. April 2003

改变的。人越老，习气越不容易改，所以要从青年人开始培养，以后才能带动各地佛教的发展。出家众是从在家众来的，只有在家众素质提高了，具有正知正见，能如理如法修学，进一步成为出家僧伽，这样的出家人才能真正住持佛法、弘法利生、绍隆佛种、续佛命脉。在法师的思想理念和人格魅力的影响下，越来越多的优秀人才特别是青年知识分子逐渐加入到僧团中来了。

▶ 2005 年 12 月 莆田广化寺常住学习班
The class for the resident monks of Putian Guanghua Monastery, December, 2005

To guide Buddhists to practice in the right way, to serve and protect Buddhism, and to benefit society, every year, Guanghua Monastery holds the Dharma Assembly for Transmitting Three Refuges, Five Precepts and Lay Bodhisattva Precepts, the Intensive Buddha Name Chanting 7-day Retreat and the Ten Thousand Buddhas Dharma Assembly with Master's personal participation and instruction. To respond to the government's call for "Humanistic Olympics, Green Olympics" and to better discover, cultivate, utilize and keep outstanding Buddhists in reserve, Master initiated the Tour of Bliss and Wisdom— Dharma Assembly of Experiencing Monastic Life during the Golden Weeks of May Day holidays and National Day holidays. Such Dharma assemblies are tailored for the young intellectuals and social elites. Through rich and varied courses, which are educational and lively, the true meaning of life is revealed at physical, psychical and spiritual levels to help young people improve their lives, purify their minds, reset their life goals and reflect upon the value of life. The Tour of Bliss and Wisdom has been held 11 times in total.

▶ 2004 年 1 月 莆田广化寺第一届福慧之旅
The 1st Tour of Bliss and Wisdom of Putian Guanghua Monastery. January 2004

　　为了引导教育广大佛教信众正确地学习佛法、护持佛法、利益社会，在法师亲自参与和指导下，广化寺每年举办"三皈五戒在家菩萨戒法会""精进佛七法会""万佛法会"等。为响应政府提出的"人文奥运、绿色奥运"之号召，为更好地发现人才、培养人才、使用和储备人才，法师还特于"五一"、"十一"黄金周期间倡办"福慧之旅——寺院生活体验营"法会，面向青年知识分子和社会精英，开展丰富多彩、寓教于乐的课程，揭示身、心、灵三个层面的生命内涵，以帮助他们改善生命、净化心灵，重新定位自己的人生目标，思考生命的价值。"福慧之旅"共举办了11届。

▶ 2007 年 10 月　莆田广化寺第十一届福慧之旅
The 11th Tour of Bliss and Wisdom of Putian Guanghua Monastery. October 2007

ii. Fufeng Famen Monastery

2. 扶风法门寺

Invited by the resident Sangha of Famen Monastery in Fufeng, Shaanxi Province, approved by Buddhist Association of Shaanxi and agreed upon by BAC, Master became the Abbot of Famen Monastery on January 16th, 2004. During the inaugural ceremony, Master said, "I have come to Famen Monastery to complete the following tasks: to fulfill my duty, to improve cooperation of Famen Monastery and lastly, to develop various Buddhist undertakings."

► 2004 年 1 月 16 日 荣膺陕西扶风法门寺住持
Inaugurated as Abbot of Fufeng Famen Monastery, Shaanxi. January 16th, 2004

Shortly after the inauguration, Master invited and appointed the new board of executives, set up a five-member leadership team and improved and completed the Monastery's regulations. At an executives' meeting, when difficulties in the Monastery's reconstruction were discussed, Master pointed out, "Such matters, which are tangible and non-lasting are easy to cope with. At the moment, our most important duty is to cultivate outstanding monks. We cannot afford a moment's delay."

On April 11th and May 22nd, 2004, with the highest level of Buddhist rituals, Master led the resident Sangha at Famen Monastery in a reception held in honor of President Hu Jintao, the Secretary-General of the CPC Central Committee, and the 11th Panchen Erdeni, the spiritual leader of Tibetan Buddhism. From May 25th to June 5th of the same year, when Shakyamuni Buddha's finger sharira which was enshrined in Famen Monastery

　　应陕西扶风法门寺常住两序大众的礼请，经陕西省佛教协会批准，上报中国佛教协会同意，法师于 2004 年 1 月 16 日荣膺法门寺住持。在晋院仪式上，法师表示："我来法门寺的任务：第一是做好工作，第二是搞好法门寺的团结，第三是发展佛教的各项事业。"

▶　2004 年 1 月 16 日 荣膺陕西扶风法门寺住持
Inaugurated as Abbot of Fufeng Famen Monastery, Shaanxi. January 16th, 2004

　　晋院后不久，法师就礼请了新一任执事，成立了五人领导小组，并进一步完善了寺院各项管理制度。在一次执事会上，大家谈及寺院改扩建工程遇到的困难时，法师说："这些有形有相的生灭法都好办，目前真正需要的是人才建设，这一点刻不容缓。"

　　2004 年 4 月 11 日和 5 月 22 日，法师在法门寺率两序大众以佛教最高礼仪，先后接待了前来视察和指导工作的中共中央总书记、国家主席胡锦涛和西藏佛教精神领袖十一世班禅大师。同年 5 月 25 日至 6 月 5 日，法门寺佛指舍利被迎请到香港供奉十日，法师担任

▶ 2004 年 5 月 在佛指舍利赴香港供奉期间接受记者采访
An interview during the period when the Buddha's finger sharira
sent to Hong Kong for worshipping. May 2004

was invited deferentially to Hong Kong for a 10-day worshipping, Master was Deputy
Chief of the Escorting Delegation. During his stay in Hong Kong, Master participated in
a number of interviews with the media including Phoenix TV and *Ta Kung Pao* of Hong
Kong. He said at an interview, "The visit of Shakyamuni Buddha's finger sharira to Hong
Kong is a great event for Buddhism with inconceivably good motivations, inconceivably
good causations, inconceivably good merits and inconceivably good results."

In order to further consolidate the good practice and study ethos, Master organized
classes, lectures and Dharma assemblies. Meanwhile, in accordance with what was set up
by the Buddha, he advocated and resumed the bimonthly precepts chanting. On June 7th,
2004, he also led the Sangha of Famen Monastery to hold the Monastery's first summer
retreat since the restoration of religious policy in the country. Through these measures, a
pure and harmonious Sangha community has been formed and a new chapter of upholding
the Dharma and perpetuating the Buddha wisdom has begun. In the summer retreat

▶ 2004 年 5 月 22 日　在法门寺与第十一世班禅大师交流
Talking with the 11th Panchen Erdeni at Famen Monastery. May 22nd, 2004

迎送团副团长。期间法师接受了香港凤凰卫视、《大公报》等多家新闻媒体的采访。在接受采访时，法师说："佛指舍利出访香港，是一件发心不可思议、因缘不可思议、功德不可思议、果报不可思议的佛门盛事。"

为进一步稳固道风学风建设，依照佛制，法师在开设学习班、举办讲座、举办法会的同时，还倡导恢复了每半月诵戒的制度，并率领大众于 2004 年 6 月 7 日，举行了自国家恢复宗教政策以来法门寺的首次结夏安居。通过这些措施，建立起了清净和合的僧团，谱写出住持正法、续佛命脉的新篇章。法师在安居的一次开示中提

▶ 2005 年 11 月 法门寺佛指舍利赴韩国供奉恭送法会
The Dharma Assembly for Escorting the Buddha's Finger Sharira to Korea for Worshipping, Famen Monastery. November 2005

Dharma talk, Master said, "We will provide training courses right after this summer retreat in order to uplift the quality of our resident Sangha. Later we will establish a Buddhist college with diverse curriculums to promote Buddhism of all the three language families and of all the eight sects of Han Buddhism." Since then, the summer retreat has been held every year. From August 29th to September 5th, 2004, Master presided over the Ullambana Universal Delivery Dharma Assembly and the First Dharma Assembly for Transmitting Three Refuges, Five Precepts and the Lay Bodhisattva Precepts, which was attended by over 1,000 people. On November 11th, 2004, the very day of Medicine Buddha's Birthday, the Buddhist Class of Famen Monastery was set up under Master's guidance.

At the invitation of the Association of Korean Buddhist Orders, Shakyamuni Buddha's finger sharira of Famen Monastery, was worshipped in Korea for 42 days from November 11th to December 20th, 2005. Master was the Chief of the Escorting Delegation. In his speech given at the set-off ceremony, Master said, "On this special occasion, which occurs once in a thousand years, all living beings are pleased. Amidst this bliss of escorting Buddha's finger sharira to Korea for worshipping, let us be bathed in the auspicious light of Buddha's compassion and wisdom, and accumulate great merits for the peace

▶ 2005 年 1 月 13 日　在法门寺为信众传授皈依
Transmitting refuges to believers at Famen Monastery. January 13th, 2005

到："安居结束后就办培训班，先提高寺院内部僧人素质，以后再办佛学院，将来要并弘三大语系、八大宗派，开设多种课程。"以后每年均举行结夏安居。同年 8 月 29 日至 9 月 5 日，法师主持了"盂兰盆普度法会暨第一届传授在家三皈五戒菩萨戒法会"，共千余人参加。11 月 11 日，适逢药师佛圣诞，法门寺佛学班在法师的精心指导下成立。

应韩国佛教宗团协议会邀请，2005 年 11 月 11 日至 12 月 20日，法门寺佛指舍利被迎请到韩国供奉 42 天，法师担任中国佛教代表团迎归团团长。他在恭送仪式上发表讲话："千载一时，因缘殊胜，众生欢喜，在这佛指舍利即将赴韩国供奉的无量法喜中，让我们共同沐浴在佛陀慈悲、智慧的吉祥之光当中，为人类的和平与进步事业多做功德。此次盛举必定为进一步巩固中韩两国佛教界

and advancement of human beings. This grand event will undoubtedly consolidate and enhance the precious 'Golden Tie' between Chinese and Korean Buddhist societies." Master remarked in the Welcome-back and Re-enshrinement Dharma Assembly, "The traditional friendship between China and Korea and various kinds of good relationships between Chinese and Korean people will certainly be consolidated and enhanced and bring more substantive benefits to the two peoples."

▶ 2006 年 5 月 1 日 中国法门寺与韩国道诜寺结为 "友好兄弟寺院"
The Joining of Famen Monastery of China and Doseonsa Temple of Korea as Brother Monasteries.
May 1st, 2006

On February 17th, 2006, Soe Win, the Prime Minister of Burma, together with over 40 people, visited Famen Monastery. On April 24th, 2006, Ratnasiri Wickramanayake, the Prime Minister of Sri Lanka, led a 9-member delegation in visiting Famen Monastery. When invited by the Prime Minister to Sri Lanka to exchange Buddhist cultures, Master replied, "The exchanges between Chinese and Sri Lankan Buddhism could date back to early days. I've been to Sri Lanka three times and was given a great reception by both the government and the Buddhist society. We are predestined to meet here at Famen Monastery today." On May 17th, 2006, Famen Monastery and Doseonsa Temple in Korea established Brother-Monasteries relationship. Witnessed by over 800 people, Master

的'黄金纽带'关系起到巨大的促进作用。"在迎归安奉法会上，法师说："中韩两国的传统友谊，以及中韩两国人民种种的友好关系，必将会得到进一步的加强和发展，为两国人民带来更多真实的利益。"

▶ 2006 年 2 月 17 日 在法门寺接待缅甸总理梭温先生
Receiving Soe Win, Prime Minister of Burma at Famen Monastery. February 17th, 2006

　　2006 年 2 月 17 日，缅甸总理梭温先生一行 40 多人访问法门寺。同年 4 月 24 日，斯里兰卡总理维克勒·马纳亚克先生一行 9 人访问法门寺，总理邀请法师去斯里兰卡进行佛教文化交流，法师说："中斯佛教友好交往历史悠久，我先后去贵国访问过三次，受到贵国政府和佛教界高规格的欢迎。今天在法门寺能见到你们，我们很有缘。"同年 5月 17 日，中国法门寺与韩国道诜寺缔结"友好兄弟寺院"。在 800 多

Xuecheng and Ven. Master Sunmook Hyeja, the Abbot of Doseonsa Temple, signed and exchanged documents.

On May 22nd, 2006, Master together with the resident Sangha, welcomed the delegation headed by Blo Bzang Vjig Med Thub Bstan Chos Dyi Nyi Ma Rinpoche, who is a member of the NPC Standing Committee and Vice President of BAC. Master said, "Theravada Buddhism and Mahayana Buddhism share the same origin with Tibetan Buddhism. We come down in one continuous line. Only when we advance side by side, endeavor jointly in a spirit of cooperation, can Buddhism as a whole be developed and strengthened harmoniously. We all worship the Foundamental Teacher Shakyamuni Buddha, transmit the Buddha's peaceful doctrines of compassion, wisdom, equality and perfect harmony and share the same goal of purifying people's minds, benefiting society and striving for peace in the world."

From July 19th to July 24th, 2006, initiated and guided by Master, the First Light of Famen Bliss and Wisdom Camp was successfully held. The Light of Famen Camp provided an opportunity for people to learn and experience Buddhism. The purpose of the Camp was to help young people reset their life goals and reflect upon the value of life. Focusing on the principle of purifying minds, the Camp provided rich and varied courses that were educational and lively, such as, "A Tour of the Monastery", "How to Lead a Happy Life", "Experiencing Sitting Meditation", "The Rules of Karma", "Happy Life Forum", "Q&A Session", "Film Appreciation", "Lamp-passing Evening", etc. The programs worked to help young people understand themselves and society, to take hold of their life and their future, to know Buddhism and to purify their minds.

At the opening ceremony of the 2nd Light of Famen Camp on July 19th, 2007, Master said, "When we encounter problems and difficulties in our daily lives, we quite often blame the outside environment. We think that our problems are caused by others' unreasonable arrangement. It is difficult for us to find the causes within ourselves. However, the Teachings of Buddha tell us that we must look into the depths of our minds to find the causes and solutions for all our problems. The Teachings of Buddha have been passed on from generation to generation. They are experiences that can provide guidance. Only under the instructions of experienced people, can we find ways to dispel afflictions, ignorance, defilements and sufferings off our minds."

人的见证下，学诚法师和韩国道诜寺方丈禅默慧慈大和尚在证书上签字并交换了文书。

2006 年 5 月 22 日，法师率两序大众迎接全国人大常委、中国佛教协会副会长嘉木样·洛桑久美·图丹却吉尼玛活佛考察团一行。法师说："南北传与藏传佛教同根同源，一脉相承，只有比肩同进，团结合作，佛教这个整体才能和合发展、进步壮大；我们信奉的都是本师释迦牟尼佛，弘扬的都是佛陀'慈悲、智慧、平等、圆融'的和平教义，目的都是净化人心、利益社会、维护世界和平。"

2006 年 7 月 19 日至 24 日，第一届"法门之光"福慧营在法师的倡导下成功举办。"法门之光"给大家创造了一个认识与体悟佛法的平台，旨在帮助年轻人重新定位自己的人生目标，思考自己的生命价值。福慧营坚持以净化为原则，结合年轻人的特点，开设了丰富多彩、寓教于乐的课程，诸如寺院巡礼、快乐人生、禅修体验、业果法则、幸福人生论坛、疑问解答、影片欣赏、传灯晚会等，以期达到"认识自我、把握人生，认识社会、把握未来，认识佛教、净化人心"的目的。

2007 年 7 月 19 日，在第二届"法门之光"的开幕式上，法师开示说："我们在现实生活当中，常常遇到问题、遇到困难，都会认为这是外境的过失，认为是别人安排不合理，不容易在自己内心当中去找原因。佛法告诉我们，所有的问题要在自己内心深处去找原因，去找解决问题的办法。佛法是一代一代传承下来的，传承下来的就是经验的指导。只有通过有经验人的指导，我们才有办法把内心的烦恼、无明、尘垢、痛苦去掉。"

In July, 2009, Master attended the 4th Light of Famen Camp and transmitted the Three Refuges to the Camp members. He also attended the first graduation ceremony of Famen Monastery Buddhist Academy and delivered a speech entitled "Be a Low Profile Person, Act in a Moderate Way and Conduct a High Profile Cultivation." He said, "Being a low-profile person means we must be modest. Acting in a moderate way is to act appropriately: too much is as bad as too little. Conducting a high-profile cultivation means having a strong sense of purpose and responsibility and putting primary energy and time in studying the Buddha's Teachings, which is the duty of monks. 'Promoting Dharma is our household task, while benefiting all sentient beings is our mission.'" By July 2011, the Light of Famen Camp had been held every summer for 6 years, with a significant and far-reaching influence.

▶ 2006 年 7 月　法门寺第一届法门之光
The 1st Light of Famen Camp of Famen Monastery. July 2006

　　2009 年 7 月，法师前往出席第四届"法门之光"福慧营，并为学员传授皈依，同时出席了法门寺佛学院首届学僧毕业典礼并发表了题为"做人要低调　做事要中调　修行要高调"的讲话。法师说："做人要低调，就是说我们要谦虚。做事要中调，就是说要恰到好处，过犹不及。修行要高调，就是我们要有很强的责任感、使命感，要把主要的精力和时间用在学佛法、弘扬佛法这个出家人的本分上，'弘法是家务，利生是事业'。""法门之光"于每年夏季举办一次，至 2011 年 7 月，已举办六届，影响深远。

▶ 2011 年 7 月　法门寺第六届法门之光
The 6th Light of Famen Camp of Famen Monastery. July 2011

On May 9th, 2009, during Master's abbotship, Famen Monastery held another millennium event, the Ceremony for the Enshrinement of Shakyamuni Buddha's Finger Sharira. Master hosted the ritual and received the sharira to be permanently enshrined and worshipped at Famen Monastery. Despite a moderate rain during the Enshrinement Dharma Assembly, Master walked peacefully with his palms pressed together all the time.

► 2009 年 5 月 9 日 在法门寺佛指舍利安奉大典上
At the Ceremony for the Enshrinement of Shakyamuni Buddha's Finger Sharira at Famen Monastery.
May 9th, 2009

During the Enshrinement Dharma Assembly, Master said, "This Buddha's finger sharira is a genuine relic of Shakyamuni. Therefore it is one of the most sacred relics worshipped by Buddhists all over the world and a valuable cultural treasure for China. It is extraordinarily meaningful that we enshrine Buddha's sharira today in the dignified stupa. This is not only a grand event for Chinese Buddhists, but for all Buddhists around the world. This event is inspired by the merits and virtues of the fourfold Buddhist assembly and is a sign of a prosperous nation, content people, a stable political situation and a harmonious society. It signifies the prosperity of the Chinese nation. It bears utmost significance in manifesting Buddha's spirits and spreading his compassion and wisdom."

　　2009 年 5 月 9 日，在法师的主持下，法门寺迎来了又一千年盛事——佛指舍利安奉大典。法师亲自主持、迎请佛指舍利永久性安奉在法门寺。安奉法会期间，天空下着小到中雨，法师一直双手合十，泰然走在雨中。

▶ 2009 年 5 月 9 日　在法门寺佛指舍利安奉大典上
At the Ceremony for the Enshrinement of Shakyamuni Buddha's Finger Sharira at Famen Monastery. May 9th, 2009

　　在安奉法会上，法师说："佛指舍利是佛陀的真身舍利，是全世界佛教信徒仰止崇拜的至高圣物，也是中华民族弥足珍贵的文化珍宝。今天，佛指舍利安座于外观庄严的舍利塔内，意义非凡。这不仅是中国佛教徒的一件盛事，也是世界佛教徒的一件盛事！这是佛教四众弟子之福德所感，是国泰民安、政通人和之标志，也是中华民族兴旺发达之象征！这对于彰显佛祖精神，传播佛陀慈悲和智慧，有着极为重要的意义。"

Master told his disciples after the Dhrama Assembly, "At that time when I was walking, all sorts of feelings surged up. Over one thousand years ago, in the Tang Dynasty, the sharira was welcomed 6 times and sent back twice, each time by a different emperor. Finally, it was enclosed in the underground palace by Emperor Xizong (862—888 AD). On the day of Buddha's birthday in 1987, the sharira reemerged after a 1,113-year disappearance. Since then, the sharira has been sent to many countries and regions around the globe such as Thailand, Korea, China's Taiwan and Hong Kong, etc., worshipped by almost 10 million people. Due to security concerns and many other considerations, the government and the Monastery have not openly enshrined the sharira in the underground palace of Famen Monastery. Now, the time has come and the conditions are met. There are absolutely causes and conditions underlying behind, innumerable causes and conditions."

Master is known to teach through action before giving verbal explanations and always be consistent in words and action. Whenever he is in the Monastery, Master, with no exception, attends the morning and evening recitations and has regular meals in the refectory. Even if he goes to bed as late as 1 a.m., he will still attend the morning recitations. Once, Master was not feeling well and his doctor told him not to attend the morning recitation, yet he still got up on hearing the beating of the board. He explained, "Sluggishness and laziness are hard to get rid of once they become habits." As for his meals, the chef monk was afraid that Master might not be used to the Northwest cuisine since he came from South China and proposed to cook separately for Master. Master declined, saying, "I've never had such a privilege." When the attendant asked if he would enjoy eating steamed bread as a Southerner, Master smiled and said, "I will eat whatever is cooked. 'When in Rome, do as the Romans do.'" The dress Master wears is simple and natural. Once in 2004, the attendant found Master's robe worn out, and intended to get Master a new one. Master heard of it and said, "No need. This robe has been with me for 15 years till now (2004), ever since I became Abbot in 1989." A few patches were made later and the robe continued to be in use. To this, the attendant sighed to himself. "The robe is indeed worthy of the name, 'Kasaya'." (A Kasaya originally refers to a robe patched by small pieces of cloth together.)

People attributed the rapid development of Famen Monastery to Master's merits and virtues, however, Master said, "It's the result of everyone's aspirations and efforts." Under this young elder's leadership, Famen Monastery is sure to regain its past glory and witness brilliance in the days to come!

法会圆满结束之后，法师告诉弟子们："当时，我这一路走来，百感交集。一千多年前的唐朝，八位皇帝，六迎二送佛指舍利，最终由唐僖宗将真身舍利封入地宫。1987年佛诞日，沉寂了1113年的真身指骨舍利重现人间！这期间，舍利虽然出访过泰国、韩国、中国台湾、中国香港等国家和地区，接受近千万人的瞻仰，但是，寺院和政府考虑安全等多种因素，始终没有公开将舍利安奉于法门寺地宫。如今众缘和合。这里面绝对是有因缘，有无量的因缘。"

身教先行、言教相随是法师一贯的风范。只要在寺院，法师每日必坚持上殿、过堂，即便是凌晨一点多才休息，第二天也依然上殿。有一次因身体欠佳，医生叮嘱不能上殿，可法师第二天仍然闻板起床，他说："养成懈怠懒惰的习气，以后不好改。"在饮食上，典座法师怕他不习惯西北的饮食，想为他单独做饭，他却说："我从来没开过小灶。"有一次用斋时，侍者问他："师父您是南方人，吃馒头习惯吗？"他笑着说："做什么吃什么，入乡随俗嘛。"他衣着朴素大方，有一次侍者发现他的袈裟破旧了，准备为他再请一件新的，他知道后认真地说："不需要，我从1989年当方丈至今（2004年），这件袈裟跟随我整整15年了。"后来又补了好几个地方继续穿，侍者暗自叹道，这才是名符其实的"袈裟"。

看着如今法门寺的迅速成长，有人说这是法师的功德，但他却说："这是大家发心承担的结果。"在这位年轻"长者"的带动下，法门寺昔日的盛况一定会早日重现，明天一定会更加辉煌！

iii. Beijing Longquan Monastery

3. 北京龙泉寺

On April 11th, 2005, upon the Buddhist devotees' hearty request and with the approval of Beijing Administration for Religious Affairs, Master became the Abbot of Beijing Longquan Monastery, which is located at the foot of the Phoenix Ridge in the Haidian District, Beijing. With aspirations of fulfilling his compassionate vows in his past lives, benefiting the capital city of Beijing and rejuvenating this ancient Monastery, Master began to preside over this 1000-year-old monastery.

At the ceremony issuing the certificate to Longquan Monastery as a legitimate religious site, Master said, "Today Longquan Monastery is reinstated as a venue for Buddhist activities. It is a day that is pleasing to Buddha, the deities and to mankind, especially the Buddhists of Beijing." Ven. Master Chuanyin, President of the Buddhist Association of Beijing, expressed his anticipation, "With Ven. Master Xuecheng as the Abbot, Longquan Monastery will certainly play a leading role in purging away defilements and bringing forth innovation. It is sure to become the capital's model Buddhist Monastery." Having been deserted for almost a century, Longquan Monastery once again regained its vitality. Even the long gone spring water (Longquan, or the Dragon Spring) has a limpid stream running again! Later on, Master reflected, "When I came to Beijing in 1984, I noticed that many local lay people had to look for monasteries in other cities. I wished that I could provide them with a sacred place to study and practice Buddha's Teachings in Beijing. 21 years have passed and now such a place has come into being."

The Sangha was confronted with many challenges and difficulties immediately after the Monastery had started to function. There were only a few simple and unsophisticated wooden structures. The facilities of the Monastery such as water, electricity and heating systems and the accommodation were far from completion. The water supply for the Monastery came from the surface flow of the mountain, but during the winter, the pipes froze and water had to be carried from somewhere else. Practically everything in the Monastery, from the infrastructure to the construction of the Sangha started out with nothing. The successful construction could not have been achieved without Master's painstaking planning and organizing efforts. Understanding that the restoration and reopening of Longquan Monastery would have profound influence on Haidian District, Beijing, the nation, Buddhism and all living beings, Master never retreated, despite the difficulties. Instead, with great will power, he confronted new challenges and ushered in a new era for the Monastery.

2005 年 4 月 11 日，在众善信殷重祈请下，经北京市宗教局批准，法师乘宿悲愿，怀着振锡北京、重兴古刹的心情，来到位于北京市海淀区凤凰岭上的龙泉寺，住持起这座有着千年历史的古刹。

在颁发宗教活动场所证书的仪式上，法师说："今天龙泉寺恢复为佛教活动场所，佛菩萨欢喜、人天欢喜，更是北京广大佛弟子欢庆的日子。"北京市佛教协会会长传印长老说："本寺由学诚法师住持，必将起到涤瑕荡垢、推陈出新的良好效果！必将使龙泉寺成为首都模范道场。"冷落近百年之宝刹，忽欣欣然又发朝气；久已断流之龙泉，复又涌出涓涓清流！法师后来说："我 1984 年来到北京时，观察当地居士们的情况，发现不少居士要跑到外地去找道场。那时，我就有个愿望，希望在北京提供给大家一个学佛的场所，提供给大家一个修行的宝地。21 年后的今天，因缘终于成熟。"

僧团入住后，一系列问题与困难迎面而来：这里只有几间古朴的木架构建筑，水、电、暖等一系列基础设施都不完善，食宿条件也都很简单。寺院用水来自山地地表径流，进入冬季后，输水管冻结，僧众只能到其他地方抬水、挑水。从寺院的各项基础设施建设到僧团建设，一切都要从零开始，无不要由法师操心策划、组织，其中的艰辛程度可想而知。但法师深知龙泉寺的恢复与开放无论对海淀、对北京，还是对国家、对社会、对佛教、对众生，都将有深远的意义与影响，所以法师从不遇难而退，反而会以更强猛的心力面对新的挑战，迎接新的开始。

The cultivation of talents is currently the priority for Buddhist society. For over a decade, Master has been considering and exploring favorable conditions for creating and cultivating an excellent Sangha. Master once said in an interview, "I am deeply aware that we are confronted with the challenges of building a Sangha in this new era and allowing Bhikshus to glorify and succeed the lineage of the Unequaled Teacher, to maintain and perpetuate the wisdom of the World Honored One in these new conditions. With today's advanced technology and abundant information, the boundary between monasteries and the outside world is minimal and nearly nonexistent. Monasteries have merged with the rest of society. All sorts of information seep into monasteries through the Internet, radio, newspapers, magazines and various events. Under such circumstances, how do Bhikshus consolidate their determination of cultivation? How do they accumulate their inner merits, virtues and strength continuously in study, contemplation and practice of Buddha's Teachings while being able to cope with the intrusions from society and dealing with lots of practical matters in such a commercialized world? In other words, how can they guarantee the tradition of uninterrupted study, contemplation and practice of Buddha's Teachings, and also the diligent cultivation of precept, concentration and wisdom, so as to keep a tranquil and peaceful mind? How can they, at the same time, shoulder the responsibilities of benefiting living beings, carrying on Buddha's work, caring the society and serving the masses according to the needs of the society. Monastics today are faced with all these tremendous challenges. Only through building a pure and harmonious Sangha, having sufficient precautionary measures in place and keeping monasteries in full function, can we meet such challenges."

Moved and inspired by Master's compassion, wisdom, aspiration and action, Longquan Monastery has formed a new type of Sangha out of nothing, which continues to grow

▶ 2006 年 12 月 3 日　在北京龙泉寺早课上
At the morning recitation of Beijing Longquan Monastery. December 3rd, 2006

　　培养人才是当前佛教界的首要任务。十几年来，法师一直在思考与探索如何营造一个培育僧才的良好环境。法师曾在一次接受采访时说："我深深地体会到：在新的时代、新的时空因缘条件下，我们怎么样来组建僧团，特别是我们出家的比丘僧在新的因缘条件下，怎么样来绍隆佛种、续佛慧命、成就佛教的事业，这里面临很多问题。比如说现在科技这么发达，资讯也这么发达，出家人的寺庙与外界可以说已经没有隔离了，寺庙和外在的社会可以说已经融为一体，就是说社会上的种种的信息不知不觉地就会传播到寺庙里来。比方说通过网络、收音机、报纸、各种各样的刊物、各种各样的活动等等。出家的比丘怎么样来巩固自己的道心，怎么样在佛法的闻思修上能够不断增长自己内在的功德、内在的力量，同时又有这种能力来应对社会上的各种资讯对我们出家人道心的侵袭；同时在这样一个商业社会，出家人又要承担很多的事务。因此既要保证出家人闻思修不间断的传统，同时又要勤修戒定慧，要寂静、安乐。另一方面，又要普度众生、承担如来的家业，关心社会、服务众生、走进人群。所以对现代的出家人来讲，挑战是很大的。只有建立一个清净和合的僧团，只有把寺庙的各种防范措施做得比较到位，只有寺庙里面的各种功能比较具足，才能应对这些挑战。"

　　在法师悲、智、愿、行之力的感召下，龙泉寺新型僧团从无到有、从小到大成长起来。进入寺院的僧众都经过严格挑选，在信心、道心、文化程度、组织观念、集体观念等各方面都比较优秀。法师

and develop. Its members have all been carefully selected and are agreeable in terms of faith, determination for cultivation, educational background, sense of organization and team spirit. Master said, "It is the man that can exalt the Way, not vice versa. Top priority should be given to the cultivation of monks. This calls for the building of a pure, harmonious and progressive Sangha of proper size with good ethos of study and practice. The Sangha, rooted deeply in upholding precepts, should have a complete educational system for the study and practice of Buddha's Teachings with a corresponding administration to ensure its smooth operation. A successful education system will allow the Sangha to continuously practice Buddha's Teachings. People of the present and future will also be able to advance their pursuits at the Monastery. Thus Buddha Dharma can be passed on from generation to generation without interruption."

▶ 2005 年 5 月 8 日 北京龙泉寺安居前结界
Territory reserving ritual before the summer retreat of Beijing Longquan Monastery. May 8th, 2005

说："'人能弘道，非道弘人'，必须把培养人才放在第一位。这就必须建立清净、和合、增上的正法僧团，要有很浓厚的学修氛围，并且还要有一定的规模。僧团要以持戒为根本，并且要有一套完整的学制，形成一个学修体系。僧团的学修体系中，要配合有相应的管理制度来保证僧团的正常运作，这是僧众能够长期持续在佛法上用功的有力保证。不仅是让现在的人，而且让以后的人都能够在这个道场里一直往上走，这样佛法才能够代代相传，经久不衰。"

▶ 2011 年 8 月 13 日　在北京龙泉寺安居自恣后合影
A group photo after the pravarana ritual at the end of summer retreat of Beijing Longquan Monastery.
August 13th, 2011

Since 2005, every year the Monastery has organized the monastic summer retreat. During the 2006 summer retreat, Master scheduled concentrated courses on precepts and supporting courses for disciples. He went to the Monastery every day to give lessons in person. He instructed the Sangha, "The focus of the Retreat is to seclude ourselves from the outside world, guard the sensory faculties, cultivate our desire for and delight in the precepts as well as our deep faith in the Three Jewels. Precepts are fundamental to perpetuating the Dharma and essential to achieving Unsurpassable Bodhi." In addition to guiding the Sangha in an in-depth study of the connotation and purposes of precepts, Master instructed his disciples on how to analyze and uphold the precepts according to different situations in actual practice and life. The whole Sangha, taking the precepts as their teacher, has become pure and harmonious and achieved great progress.

With respect to management, Master far-sightedly established the ethics model of the Sangha by referring to the traditional Vinaya's Karma system and modern monastic management experiences. The members of the Sangha follow two ethics: one based on the different precepts received, the other based on the administrative system.

According to the precepts received, a monk's seniority is based on the levels and the time when they receive precepts. There are three different levels of precepts for Bhikshus, Shramaneras and Postulants in the descending order. Within each level, the seniority is based on the time of receiving precepts, the earlier the senior. All religious activities like morning and evening recitations, eating meals together at refectory, chanting sutras, doing Uposatha and so on are arranged by the ethics in precepts. In the ascending order of Postulant, Shramanera and Bhikshu, the junior monks should respect and learn from the seniors and the senior monks should care for and guide the junior ones. Administrative ethics are based on administrative positions. In performing duties, members of lower positions should obey those of higher positions. Those who do not have positions should obey executives, while senior members should strictly discipline themselves and set examples through their own actions to assist the growth and improvement of the members at lower positions rather than acting as officials. These two types of ethics are each applicable in different situations and should not be confused. Neither system should be abused or neglected. If each member of the Sangha can perfectly understand his role and perform his responsibilities accordingly, the Sangha will be strongly bound together.

从 2005 年开始，寺院每年均举行结夏安居。在 2006 年结夏安居期间，法师为弟子们规划了密集的戒律课程和相关的辅助课程，并每日回到寺内亲自授课。他教导僧众："在安居期间，重点是摒弃外缘、收摄身心，培养对戒律的好乐心以及对三宝的深厚信念。戒律是正法久住的根本，成就无上菩提的道基。"除了每晚带领僧众深入学习戒律的内涵和意趣，法师还着重教授弟子如何将所学戒律结合实际修学生活的状况进行分析、抉择。全寺上下，以戒为师，清净和合，个人及整体都有明显的进步。

在管理方面，法师高瞻远瞩，参照戒律羯磨制度以及现代丛林管理的经验，确立了僧团伦理规范：僧团成员遵循戒别和行政两种伦理。

依戒别高低的伦理以受戒的程度和先后来区分，受戒程度从高到底分比丘、沙弥和净人三个层次，同一个层次里依戒腊，即受戒的先后排序。上殿、过堂、诵经、布萨等宗教活动的位次都要依着戒别伦理。以净人、沙弥、比丘之序，下座对上座要恭敬、学习；上座对下座要关心、引导。行政伦理即依行政职务的高低，在做事时就要依着行政系统，下位服从上位，清众服从执事。下位成员虚心向上位成员学习，接受教导和劝诫，上位成员严格要求自己，以身作则，照顾帮助下位成员的成长和提升；执事对清众要以身教为先，不可有当官的心态。两种伦理各有适用的场合，不能混淆，也不能执此废彼。总之，僧团的每个成员都能够安立好自己的角色，敦伦尽分，一个僧团就能够有很强的和力。

Master has arranged for young members of the Sangha to learn and recite traditional cultural classics, so as to raise their morality and perfect their personality and quality as monks. Such classics include, *Rules for Disciples*, *The Confucian Analects*, *The Great Learning*, *The Universal Order*, *Mencius*, *Tao Te Ching*, *Chuang Tse*, *Anthology of Three Hundred Tang Poems*, *Best Classical Chinese Essays*, *Forty-two Chapters Sutra*, *Sutra of the Buddha's Last Teaching*, *Sutra of Eight Awareness of Great Beings* and many others.

Under the continuous exploration of Master, Longquan Monastery has inherited the best of the traditional monastic system while absorbing the characteristics of modern institutional Buddhist education. Therefore a high quality Sangha has come into shape.

According to the disciplines of the Sangha, monastics without posts cannot own cell phones. Contact with the outside world is generally not allowed unless it is necessary to do so and approved by an executive monk. Televisions, newspapers, magazines and radio are not allowed. No food is kept in the dormitory and no snack is permitted outside the refectory. No allowance is issued and money offered by devotees must be handed in to the Sangha. The Sangha provides its members with all reasonable expenses that they may need so that monks are free from all monetary concerns to secure both body and mind tranquility for study and practice...This system has ensured pure monastic practice.

All activities of the Sangha such as morning and evening recitations, attending classes, eating together at refectory, labor work, summer retreats, precepts study, Karma meetings, bimonthly precepts chanting, etc., are all conducted orderly in accordance with the Teachings and Vinaya. Moreover, monks often examine their own behaviors and correct what's not in accordance with the requirements of deportment or the Teachings. At classes, Master often leads the reading and discussion of sutras and treatises such as *Avatamsaka Sutra*, *The Treatise on Wisdom*, *Lamrim Chenmo*, and *Lecture Notes on the Four-Part Bhikshu Precepts*. Master also takes the lead in labor work. In June, 2006, to solve the water shortage, he led the Sangha and laity disciples up to the source dike of the mountain stream and dredged up the accumulated silt and sands.

对年纪轻的出家众，法师特别安排他们学习背诵《弟子规》《论语》《大学》《中庸》《孟子》《道德经》《庄子》《唐诗三百首》《古文观止》《四十二章经》《佛遗教经》《八大人觉经》等传统文化经典，以提高道德素养，促进人格、僧格的完善。

在法师的不断总结摸索下，龙泉寺僧团既继承了传统丛林的精华，又汲取了现代佛学院教育的特点，形成了高素质的僧团。

僧团规定：清众不拥有手机，平时不准对外联系，需要联系时，申报执事法师批准方可；不看电视、报纸、杂志，不收听广播；寮房内不存食物，斋堂外不吃零食；不发单资，傥钱入公，僧团保证个人一切合理开销，解决僧众的一切后顾之忧，保证在学修时身心安定……合理的制度保证了僧众的清净修行。

僧众上殿、上课、过堂、出坡、安居、学戒、羯磨、半月诵戒等各项活动，如法如律、秩序井然。大家还经常自我检查和纠正平日言谈举止中不合威仪、不如法的地方。在课堂上，法师常带领大家一起读诵、研究经论，如《华严经》《大智度论》《菩提道次第广论》《四分律比丘戒本讲义》等。法师还带头出坡劳动，2006 年 6 月，为了解决用水紧张的问题，他亲自带领僧俗弟子，上山到山涧的源头水坝处，清挖淤泥积沙。

▶ 2006 年 6 月 24 日 视察北京龙泉寺后山水库
Going to the reservoir on the back hill of Beijing Longquan Monastery. June 24th, 2006

As long as Master stays at a monastery, he leads the morning and evening recitations of the Sangha, and there is no exception at Longquan Monastery. Master said, "The purity and harmony of the Sangha depends on the right view, precepts, and practice in accordance with the Teachings. Such practice relies on an individual cultivation, regular practice, and aspiration to work for the Sangha and benefit others. Without regular practice, it is nearly impossible to be beneficial toward others." He continued, "You shall be closer than brothers. We take the same path, we practice together and we learn with each other. I am your teacher, your friend as well as your fellow practitioner."

Guided by Master's instructions and his personal example, the Sangha's study, cultivation and work are so directed as to help "cultivate the mind through real-life encounters". They manage to combine their scriptural study, contemplation and practice with the cultivation of precepts, concentration and wisdom. In this way, they can integrate well the issues such as the understanding of the doctrine and the true life, the Buddha Dharma and mundane dharma, self-cultivation and team development, and benefiting oneself as well as others. The spirit of "Six Harmonies" in the Sangha has been gradually fostered by unifying views, establishing common understandings, upholding pure precepts, living in harmony, putting equal emphasis on study

▶ 2007 年 8 月 16 日 在北京龙泉寺出坡栽竹子
Planting bamboos at Beijing Longquan Monastery. August 16th, 2007

　　只要在寺院，法师就会坚持上殿领众熏修，在龙泉寺自然也不例外。法师说："僧团清净和合，在于知见、戒律、如法行持；行持在于个人修行用功、定课及发心承担、利他。个人无定课，谈利他不太可能。""你们在一起，应比兄弟还亲，同道、同参、同学，我们亦师亦友亦学人。"

　　在法师言传身教下，僧团通过学习、修行、做事，历境练心，将"闻、思、修"，"戒、定、慧"，理与事，佛法与世间法，个人与团队，自利与利他有机地结合起来。"六和"精神在僧团内部得以逐步实现：统一知见，建立共识；戒行清净，和合共住；学修并进，相互增上。一进僧团，即能感受到纯正的道风及浓厚的学

and practice and helping each other. As soon as one is within the Sangha, he can feel the monastic ethos of an excellent learning atmosphere. The whole Sangha shows a positive spirit for integrating Buddha Dharma with life. They rely on Master to help them study and practice, they follow the Buddha's Teachings to maintain harmony and rely on fellow practitioners to make progress.

Master has stated, "Though self-improvement of the Sangha is the most essential first step," you shall not wait until you are perfectly educated to promote the Buddha's Teachings. You should learn while teaching. To teach is to learn. To educate the fourfold assembly is the primary task of the Sangha in preaching Dharma and benefiting living beings." Under the guidance of Master, Longquan Monastery began to organize various Dharma assemblies to reach Buddhist believers.

In 2005, on the eighth day of the fourth month of the lunar calendar (May 15th), Longquan Monastery held its first Bathing Buddha Dharma Assembly with about 300 participants. Master transmitted the Three Refuges to the believers and said, "Taking Refuge is not merely chanting

▶ 2010 年 5 月 21 日（农历四月初八）在北京龙泉寺浴佛法会上
At the Bathing Buddha Dharma Assembly of Beijing Longquan Monastery. May 21st (the eighth day of the fourth month of the lunar calendar), 2010

习氛围，通过依师学修、依法和合、依友增上，整个僧团呈现出佛法与生命结合后积极向上的面貌。

法师告诫大家："虽然僧团的提升是最必要的第一步，但也不可能等到学好了再去弘传，要边做边学、教学相长。四众弟子的教育是僧团弘法利生的主要工作。"在他的引导带领之下，龙泉寺开始对外举办各种法会，广泛接引信众。

2005 年农历四月初八，龙泉寺首次举办"浴佛法会"，约有 300 人参加。法师为信众传授了三皈依，并开示说："皈依不仅仅

▶ 2008 年 5 月 12 日（农历四月初八）北京龙泉寺浴佛法会暨"缅甸风暴"消灾祈福大法会
Dharma Assembly of Bathing Buddha and Praying for Blessings and Disaster Relief for Burma Storm, Beijing Longquan Monastery. May 12th (the eighth day of the fourth month of the lunar calendar), 2008

rituals and taking the Refuge Certificate home. We are disciples of the Buddha and we shall earnestly practice the Buddha's Teachings." The new Buddhists started to benefit from the Teachings and found delight in Dharma.

From the fifteenth day of the fourth month to the fifteenth day of the seventh month of the lunar calendar (May 22nd—August 19th), 2005, Longquan Monastery held its first summer retreat. During that period, all monks were refrained from going out. They set their minds on precepts study. Since then, the Karma meetings and the precepts chanting have been held every half a month in accordance with the Vinaya. On the fifteenth day of the seventh month of the lunar calendar, the last day of the 3-month summer retreat, the Ullambana Dharma Assembly was held. To prepare for the Dharma Assembly, Master returned to Longquan Monastery almost every day from the Buddhist Association of China to guide the Sangha and laity. At the concluding meeting, Master encouraged everyone by saying, "As long as we have the right motivation and take the promotion of Buddhism and the elimination of all living beings' sufferings as our mission, we will certainly be empowered by all Buddhas. Both the Sangha and the laity should act in accordance with the Dharma, do real work for Buddhism and contribute to the harmony of the society."

On the nineteenth day of the ninth month of the lunar calendar (October 21st), 2005, the date on which Avalokiteshvara Bodhisattva renounced the secular life, Longquan Monastery held a 3-day Lotus Sutra Dharma Assembly. Master transmitted Three Refuges at the request of the devotees. He appreciated their great virtues that led them to take refuge in Buddhism and in the Three Jewels. Master said, "Longquan Monastery will hold itself responsible for all believers who take refuge here. We will continue to have Dharma assemblies in the future and provide courses and opportunities for devotees to study and practice Buddha's Teachings."

From the first day to fourteenth day of the first month of the lunar calendar (January 29th—February 11th), 2006, Longquan Monastery organized the Spring Festival Blessings and Flower Adornment Sutra Dharma Assembly. Over 1,000 people celebrated the Chinese New Year at the Monastery. On the fifth day, Master transmitted Three Refuges and Eight Precepts to over 200 believers in the chilly open yard. At the concluding meeting of the Sangha, Master said, "In the past year, all of you have worked hard. You have encountered many challenges, but you have faced them and resolved them. This is indeed gratifying!"

Following the Flower Adornment Sutra Dharma Assembly, Longquan Monastery organized many rich and diverse Dharma activities in 2006, including the Lotus Sutra Dharma Assembly, Ullambana Dharma Assembly and the Mid-Summer Universal

是念一遍仪轨把皈依证拿回去就可以了。我们是佛门弟子，要按照佛法去身体力行。"皈依信众初蒙法益，得沾法喜。

同年农历四月十五至七月十五，寺院首次举行结夏安居，于此三月之中所有僧众禁足摄心，学习戒律，并自此以后，每半月如法羯磨，依律诵戒。农历七月十五，僧团三月结夏安居圆满并举办"盂兰盆法会"。为筹备此次法会，法师几乎每天都从中国佛教协会返回寺院，带领僧俗二众做充分的准备工作。结行会时，法师勉励大家："只要我们发心正确，真正以佛教之兴衰为己任，以天下苍生之疾苦为己任，必有诸佛加被。僧俗弟子们要如法行持，真正为佛教做实事，为社会和谐做贡献。"

农历九月十九是观世音菩萨出家日，龙泉寺举办了为期三天的"法华法会"。法师为求受皈依的信众传授了三皈依，并赞叹大家进入佛门皈依三宝的殊胜善根。法师表示："龙泉寺将对在这里皈依的信众负责，以后还将会继续举办法会，并且为信众提供学习佛法的课程以及修习的机会。"

2006年正月初一至十四，寺院举办了"迎春祈福华严法会"，上千人在寺院共度春节。初五，法师在寒风凛冽的露天会场为200多位信众传授了皈依和八关斋戒。在僧众总结会上，法师说："一年来，诸位同学都付出了辛勤的劳动，从中也碰到不少境界，你们都能够去面对与解决，十分可喜！"

在法师悲心愿力的摄持下，以"华严法会"为起点，2006年全年，寺院又举办了"法华法会""盂兰盆法会""中元普度法会"等

Salvation Dharma Assembly. During each Dharma assembly, Master transmitted Three Refuges and Eight Precepts to believers and guided them to Buddhism. A succession of Buddhist cultural events was held during the Golden Weeks of May Day and National Day holidays to demonstrate the active engagement of Buddhism in the secular world and the delivery of all living beings. As time goes by, more and more believers come to attend the Dharma assemblies, which enable the Dharma assemblies to gradually grow in size and influence.

▶ 2010 年 5 月 21 日 在北京龙泉寺与新皈依弟子
Master and the disciples newly taking refuges, Beijing Longquan Monastery. May 21st, 2010

Thanks to Master's efforts, the conditions for organizing Dharma assemblies have greatly improved. Since 2007, the Monastery has regularly held the following Dharma assemblies every year: The Flower Adornment Sutra Chanting Dharma Assembly, in the period of Chinese New Year; The Wonderful Dharma Lotus Flower Sutra Chanting Dharma Assembly to celebrate the birthday of Avalokiteshvara Bodhisattva, on the nineteenth day of the second month of the lunar calendar; Ksitigarbha Sutra Chanting Dharma Assembly, on the Tomb-Sweeping Day; Shurangama Sutra Chanting Dharma Assembly, during the May Day holidays; the Bathing Buddha Dharma Assembly, on the eighth day of the fourth month of the lunar calendar (the birthday of Shakyamuni Buddha); The Wonderful Dharma Lotus Flower Sutra Chanting Dharma Assembly, on the

内容丰富、形式多样的法务活动。每次法会，法师都会为信众传授皈依、八关斋戒，接引众生进入佛门。特别是在"五一""十一"黄金周举办佛教文化系列活动，向社会大众展示了佛教积极入世、普度众生的精神面貌。随着时间的推移，参加法会的信众越来越多，法会规模逐渐扩大，影响越来越好。

▶ 2009 年 4 月 4 日 北京龙泉寺清明祭祖报恩法会
Dharma Assembly of Repaying the Benevolence of Ancestors on the Tomb Sweeping Day, Beijing Longquan Monastery. April 4th, 2009

在法师的精心安排下，寺院举办法会的各种因缘更加成熟。2007 年以后，寺院每年春节期间，举办诵《华严经》法会；农历二月十九观世音菩萨圣诞日，举办诵《法华经》法会；清明节，举办诵《地藏经》法会；"五一"，举办诵《楞严经》法会；农历四月初八释迦牟尼佛圣诞日，举办"浴佛法会"；农历六月十九观世音菩萨成道日，举办诵《法华经》法会；农历七月十五，僧团结夏安居

nineteenth day of the sixth month of the lunar calendar, the date on which Avalokiteshvara Bodhisattva attained enlightenment; the Ullambana Dharma Assembly, on the fifteenth day of the seventh month of the lunar calendar, the date on which the summer retreat of the Sangha is completed; the Shurangama Sutra Chanting Dharma Assembly, during the Golden Week of National Day holiday; The Wonderful Dharma Lotus Flower Sutra Chanting Dharma Assembly, on the nineteenth day of the ninth month of the lunar calendar, the date on which Avalokiteshvara Bodhisattva renounced the secular life. Starting from the Golden Week of National Day holiday of 2009, Master, responding to the new conditions, changed the function of Dharma assemblies from establishing affinity with believers to educating them. The Intensive Group Cultivation Dharma Assembly is held annually during the National Day holiday.

Master once said, "By commanding and proficiently employing various languages, we could in a way follow the example of Buddha to enlighten all living beings and promote the spread of Buddhism worldwide." The Dharma assemblies have become more customary at Longquan Monastery and a multilingual team is developing. Master therefore has initiated multilingual Dharma assemblies in January of 2011. Since then, in major Dharma assemblies at Longquan Monastery, the multilingual session covers such languages as English, French, German, Russian, Japanese, Korean, Spanish, Italian, Vietnamese, Sanskrit, Pali, Tibetan, etc.

▶ 2012 年 1 月 22 日（除夕）北京龙泉寺多语种法会 中外学员表演观世音菩萨的故事
The Chinese and foreign participants of multilingual Dharma assembly performing the story about Avalokiteshvara Bodhisattva. January 22th (Chinese New Year's Eve), 2012

竟，举办"盂兰盆法会"；"十一"黄金周，举办诵《楞严经》法会；农历九月十九观世音菩萨出家日，举办诵《法华经》法会。从2009年"十一"黄金周起，法师根据新的缘起，对法会的类型作了新的调整，将结缘型法会转变为教育型法会，每年举行"十一精进共修法会"。

法师曾说，"掌握并熟练运用各种语言文字，我们就能在某种程度上效法佛陀，让众生随类各得解，推动佛教在世界的弘扬。"随着龙泉寺法会的日渐规范化、正规化以及多语种团队的发展，从2011年元旦起，法师倡导在龙泉寺的主要法会中举办涵盖英、法、德、俄、日、韩、西班牙、意大利、越南、梵、巴利、藏等语种在内的多语种法会。

▶ 2010 年 10 月　在北京龙泉寺精进共修法会上
At the Intensive Group Practice Dharma Assembly of Beijing Longquan Monastery. October 2010

Being at their initial stage, the multilingual Dharma assemblies focus on establishing affinity connections with believers through events like morning and evening recitations, scripture chanting, Dharma talks, outdoor work, bow repentances, meditation, food serving, interactive online broadcasts, multi-cultural exchanges, teaching Buddhist songs and Buddhist film appreciation. The Dharma assemblies are designed to guide followers in lively and various ways. Master once pointed out that Buddhism would only be socialized when it is globalized. The multilingual Dharma assemblies, which serve language enthusiasts and foreigners, are an important link in this process of globalization.

Master once said to the Sangha, "Without a pure, harmonious and progressive Sangha, it is impossible to retain the Dharma, let alone to develop and promote it. You have aspired to become monks and have studied and practiced so hard. I am overjoyed that you have decided to become monks and have studied and practiced so hard. You must keep a clear vision of why you should have become monks, and what are your mission and duties. You are here not only for yourselves, but for Buddhism as a whole, for the enlightenment of living beings, and for the promotion of Dharma. Only true faith in the path that you have chosen can enable you to overcome difficulties. Now that the religions of the world have started to engage in dialogues, we should refrain from taking the sole path of one particular sect of Buddhism. On some occasions, we speak on behalf of Buddhism. You will be the successors of the whole Buddhism. We do not cultivate ordinary abbots or persons who are eloquent in Dharma preaching or skilled in doing things. We cultivate great monks and virtuous masters who have made great vows and possess great compassion, great wisdom and great conduct."

"At present, my overriding mission is to cultivate monastics and disseminate Dharma. From now on, I expect you to make great resolve and be courageous in taking responsibilities. I am here to pave the road and build the bridge for you. I will exert my every effort to assist you and help you attain achievements. We have been related since past lives and I am willing to go forth together with you through eternity. You are all blessed with better conditions than I am; your future attainments will be beyond imagination. You should have every reason to be confident with your future. You must make more efforts to maintain harmony and get improvement in spite of setbacks."

Thanks to the merits and virtues of Master, the Sangha expanded from 5 members to more than 100, the number of resident lay people rose from 1 to over 200 and more and

多语种法会初创时期，基于结缘型的定位，开展了早晚课、诵经、法师讲座、田间劳作、拜忏、静坐、行堂体验、网络直播互动、多元文化交流、佛教歌曲学唱、佛教影片赏析等活动，尝试以活泼多样的方式接引有缘信众。法师曾提出，佛教只有全球化才能真正社会化。而面向多语种爱好者及外国人的多语种法会，即是全球化过程中的重要环节。

法师教导僧众："建立正法靠的是清净和合增上的僧团，否则正法难以住世，佛法难以发扬光大。你们发心出家，又很用功，我很高兴。应知道自己出家的目的为何，知道自己的使命、责任，不仅仅是为个人，要为整个佛教，为众生法身慧命，为正法的弘扬。对自己所选择的路有笃定的信心，才能克服困难。我们不能走宗派的路子，世界宗教正在走向对话，在一些场合下，我们一说话代表的就是佛教。你们以后是整个佛教的接班人！我们培养人才，不是培养一般的住持，或会说法、会做事的人，要培养有大愿力、大慈悲、大智慧、大行为的高僧大德。"

"我现在最大的使命就是培养人才和弘法。今后，你们要发广大心，勇敢承担。我是为你们铺路搭桥的，我会用自己的一切帮助大家、成就大家。我与你们也有宿世的缘分，很愿意同诸位一起走下去，直至永远。诸位的条件都比我好，未来的成就是不可思议的。你们要相信自己的未来，从而更加努力、和合、辗转增上。"

由于法师自身功德的感召，僧团已从最初的 5 人发展到现在的 100 多人，常住居士也由最初的 1 人发展到现在的 200 多人，皈依

more believers have taken refuges here, which made the existing buildings and facilities inadequate for daily operation. Led by his great vows, Master led monastic and lay disciples to complete the construction of Longquan Reservoir, Dechen Building, Laity's Building, the Multi-functional Complex (Jianxing Hall, East Wing Building, North Wing Building), Educational Building, etc., and also the restoration of the old Buddha Hall.

Master had put great energy into the construction during its whole process from preliminary design, framework building to final decoration. Almost every day after he returned back to the Monastery from BAC, Master immediately went to the construction site to learn about the progress and give timely guidance to specific problems. He also engaged in construction work, helping workers to carry bricks and build walls. Especially in the crucial stage, Master often worked with others at the construction site all night and left behind all of his fatigue got in the daytime work at BAC. His inexhaustible energy truly demonstrates the nature of a Bodhisattva—selfless and altruistic.

On September 30th, 2009, Master talked about the guiding principles for the long-term management of Longquan Monastery at Jianxing Hall, which was newly put into use.

(1) Order of the Monastics and the Laity should be specified as (a) differentiating by the precepts received and the administrative positions held, being different from each other though inseparable, and (b) being equal by nature, yet different in specific matter.

(2) Order of Study and Practice should be specified as (a) faith, understanding, practice and attainment, in this sequence, and (b) generating Bodhicitta and extensively accumulating provisions.

(3) Order of Work should be specified as (a) conforming to the Teachings whether talking or keeping silent, moving or being still, and (b) dealing with people and things with sincerity.

(4) Order of Life should be specified as (a) the purity and dignity of daily activities involved with eating, clothing, lodging and transportation, and (b) the purification of the three karmas: body, speech and mind, and the possession of physical serenity for achieving spiritual enlightenment.

With respect to the Order of the monastics and the Laity, Master said, "The monastics and the laity are inseparable. The monastics are responsible for upholding the Buddha's

信众也越来越多。已有的建筑设施已经无法满足僧俗二众日常运转的需要。法师发大愿力，带领僧俗先后完成了龙泉水库、德尘居、居士楼、老大殿维修、多功能弘法楼——见行堂及东配楼、北配楼、教学楼等工程。

在建设过程中，从前期的设计、中期的框架结构建设到后期的装修，法师均投入了大量心血。他几乎每天从中佛协下班回寺后，都会第一时间到工地关心视察工程进展情况，及时指导解决施工时所遇到的实际困难。他还常常亲自投身于施工中，与工人一起搬砖砌墙，特别在攻坚阶段，法师常常与大家彻夜奋战在施工现场，把白天在中佛协上班的劳累全部抛于脑后。实际上，法师怎么会不累呢？这真正是在为众生示现菩萨无我利他的行境。

2009 年 9 月 30 日，法师在新启用的见行堂，开示龙泉道场有序化管理的长期方针：

(1) 僧俗有序：①戒别行政，不二而二；②理上平等，事相差别。

(2) 学修有序：①信解行证，次第分明；②发菩提心，广集资粮。

(3) 工作有序：①语默动静，如法如理；②待人接物，诚心诚意。

(4) 生活有序：①衣食住行，清净庄严；②规范三业，身安道隆。

对于僧俗有序，法师开示说："僧俗二众不可分离，出家众住持佛法，在家众护持佛法，出家人与居士必须要有良好的分工配合，各司其职，并且要形成一个和合增上的团队，形成僧俗配合传

▶ 2009 年 9 月 在北京龙泉寺东配楼建筑工地上
At the construction site of the East Wing Building, Beijing Longquan Monastery. September 2009

Teachings, while the laity are responsible for protecting and supporting the Buddha's Teachings. There should be a good division of responsibilities and collaboration between the two groups. Each of them should do their job well to form a harmonious and progressive team. Cooperation between the monastics and the lay people is necessary for transmitting and upholding Buddha Dharma. The monastics should work hard in cultivation, make progress in Dharma pursuit and guide the laity to protect and support the Sangha. Then, the monastics and the laity can cooperate with each other to promote the Buddha's Teachings. It is crucial to form such a system. Only with such a system can powerful collective karma be created, and Buddhist undertakings be completed intensively and extensively."

On October 8th, 2009, 5 departments were established in order to implement the orderly management of Longquan Monastery proposed by Master.

(1) Construction Department is in charge of the Monastery's infrastructure construction.

(2) Culture Department is responsible for editing, designing and producing the Monastery's books and media products.

(3) Charity Department, namely, Beijing Ren Ai Charity Foundation, holds the

▶ 2009 年 10 月 2 日　在北京龙泉寺见行堂开示
Giving a Dharma talk at the Jianxing Hall, Beijing Longquan Monastery. October 2nd, 2009

持佛法的模式。出家人修行、用功，在法上提升，并引导在家居士护持僧团。然后僧俗配合弘扬佛法，这个体系的形成非常关键。有了这个体系，才能够真正凝聚起强大的共业，将佛法事业做得深入、广大。"

2009 年 10 月 8 日，为具体落实法师提出的龙泉道场有序化管理的构想，寺院成立了五个部门，分别是：

（1）工程部。负责寺院的各项基础设施建设。

（2）文化部。主要负责寺院各类图书、音像制品的编辑、设计、制作和出版。

（3）慈善部。北京市仁爱慈善基金会，其宗旨是传播慈善文

mission of spreading the culture and spirit of charity and promoting the action of poverty relief. It aims to build up a platform for encouraging virtuous motivation and practicing virtuous deeds where everyone can get themselves involved. The Foundation follows the idea of "Everyone can enjoy taking part in charity work. Ren Ai charity activities are within your reach."

(4) Publicity Department is in charge of the Voice of Longquan website and Ven. Master Xuecheng's Blog. The website aims at disseminating traditional Chinese culture, the content of which covers Buddhism, Taoism and Confucianism, and concerns about various aspects of modern society. The website in Chinese, English and Japanese claims visitors from over 170 countries and regions.

(5) Department of Education consists of three divisions:

(a) The Division of Dharma Assembly aims to provide preliminary education to lay Buddhists through the organization of activities that connect the masses and proclaim the universal values of Buddhism.

(b) The Division of Student Affairs offers services and support for the study and practice of lay Buddhists through recruiting Buddhist study group members and organizing and maintaining the operation of the study groups.

(c) The Division of Instructor Affairs is to train Buddhist missionaries of the new era by educating and giving guidance to instructors of the study groups.

Other departments include Beijing Great Sinology Foundation and Translation Center of Beijing Longquan Monastery. The Foundation's main function is to provide complimentary books such as traditional Chinese classics. It also conducts domestic and overseas cultural exchanges. The Translation Center is responsible for the translation and distribution of Master's multilingual microblogs, the translation and publication of all kinds of books and media products of the Monastery. The Center also translates and interprets for relevant reception of the Monastery.

Thus the new framework of operations has been set up at the Monastery. The Sangha runs through the monastic executive system and the endeavors of spreading Dharma operate through an organizational structure.

化、弘扬慈善精神、推动扶贫救助。其目标是搭建启发善心、人人可参与的善行实践平台。其理念是"人人享有慈善，仁爱触手可及"。

（4）弘宣部。负责龙泉之声传统文化网和学诚法师的博客。网站以弘扬中华传统文化为宗旨，内容涉及释道儒等多方面，关注现代人生、社会的方方面面。中、英、日三种语言版本的网站拥有来自170多个国家和地区的读者。

（5）教化部。下设三个处：

①法会处。主要通过举办各类活动，在接引大众、宣扬佛法普世价值的基础上实现对居士的初步教育。

②学修处。主要通过学佛小组学员的招募、小组组建和维护，为居士学修提供服务和保障。

③研修处。主要通过对讲师的带动和引导，培养新时代的佛教传教士。

另有北京复兴大国学文化基金会和北京龙泉寺翻译中心。文化基金会主要向公众无偿赠送中华传统文化经典，并开展海内外文化交流活动等。翻译中心主要负责多语种微博的翻译及发布、寺院各类图书和音像制品的翻译和出版，并为寺院相关接待工作提供翻译服务。

自此形成了僧团内部按执事制度运作，弘法事业按组织架构运作的新格局。

▶ 2011 年 1 月 22 日 与北京龙泉寺讲师合影
A group photo with instructors of Beijing Longquan Monastery. January 22nd, 2011

▶ 2009 年 11 月 7 日 北京龙泉寺第一批学佛小组开班
The launching of the 1st Buddhist study groups of Beijng Longquan Monastery. November 7th, 2009

▶ 2009 年 11 月 7 日　在北京龙泉寺第一批学佛小组开班仪式上开示
Giving a Dharma talk at the opening ceremony of the 1st Buddhist study groups of Beijing Longquan Monastery. November 7th, 2009

▶ 2011 年 11 月 21 日　北京龙泉寺第十批学佛小组开班
The launching of the 10th Buddhist study groups of Beijing Longquan Monastery. November 21st, 2011

The year of 2010 witnessed the 5th anniversary of Longquan Monastery's reopening for religious services. The five years' development of the Monastery has been a vivid representation of Master's compassion and aspiration. Master's broad mind and outstanding vision had won sincere reverence from his disciples. On September 22th (the fifteenth day of the eighth month of the lunar calendar, the traditional Mid-autumn Festival), 2010, to express their profound gratitude to the virtuous teachers, the disciples held a meeting entitled "5th Anniversary Retrospect: Five Years on the Bodhi Path, Memories of Masters' Benevolence" and an evening party entitled "A Gathering on a Cool Evening to Recollect Masters' Benevolence". During the events, Master especially encouraged disciples to make more efforts in the future to serve the society and create new history.

Guided by Master, starting from October 2009, Longquan Monastery launched series of lectures under the title of Longquan Lectures. The speakers are renowned scholars and experts within and outside of China. They talk on various topics including religion, history, charity and culture. The knowledge of both the monastics and lay people are

► 2010 年 9 月 22 日（农历八月十五）在北京龙泉寺恢复宗教活动场所五周年庆典上
At the 5th Anniversary of Longquan Monastery's reopening for religious services. September 22nd (the fifteenth day of the eighth month of the lunar calendar), 2010

　　至 2010 年，龙泉寺恢复宗教活动场所已五年。五年来，寺院各方面的发展无不渗透着法师的悲心和愿力，他开放的心胸和异乎常人的远见，令弟子们深深地敬仰。9 月 22 日（农历八月十五），弟子们为了表达对师长的无限感恩，在见行堂举行了"五岁菩提路 共话师长恩——五周年回顾会"和"相聚清凉夜 共话师长恩——中秋晚会"。在活动中，法师策励弟子们未来要更加努力，服务社会，创造历史。

　　在法师的指导下，从 2009 年 10 月起，龙泉寺推展了"龙泉讲堂"系列讲座。讲演者为来自国内外的知名学者和专家，内容涉及宗教、历史、慈善、文化等多个方面。讲座丰富了僧俗二众的知识结构，开阔了视野。2011 年 8 月 14 日（农历七月十五），北京师范

▶ 2011 年 8 月 14 日（农历七月十五）在北京师范大学人文宗教高等研究院龙泉基地成立仪式上
At the opening ceremony of Longquan Temple Research Base of the Institute for Advanced Study of the Humanities and Religion, Beijing Normal University. August 14th (the fifteenth day of the seventh month of the lunar calendar), 2011

greatly enriched with a broadened view. On August 14th (the fifteenth day of the seventh month of the lunar calendar), 2011, the Institute for Advanced Study of the Humanities and Religion of Beijing Normal University established a research base at Longquan Monastery. The founding of this base was an important step forward serving as an example with far-reaching significance on the new development of the exchanges and collaboration between the religious society and the academic society.

Master has led the Monastery to make remarkable advancements both in infrastructure construction and the cultivation of monks. Longquan Monastery will surely become a platform for promoting traditional Chinese culture, a source for elevating morality and purifying minds, a link for exchanging cultures and building friendships and a sacred place to promote Buddha Dharma, benefit sentient beings and create a blessed and harmonious society. Just as Master said, "What we do today is in preparation for tomorrow. What we do this year is in preparation for next year. What we do in this life is in preparation for next life and what we do lifetime after lifetime is in preparation for attaining Buddhahood. What we have achieved is not yet ideal; what is perfect is attaining Buddhahood!"

大学人文宗教高等研究院在龙泉寺设立基地。基地的成立，朝着宗教界与学术界开创相互交流与合作的新局面，迈出了具有前瞻性、示范性的一步，势必产生深远的影响。

在法师的带领下，寺院从各项基础设施建设到优秀僧才的培养，都不断向前迈进着。龙泉寺必将成为继承与发扬传统文化的载体，提升道德、净化心灵的源头，交流文化、联结友谊的纽带，弘法利生、祥和社会的宝地。诚如法师所说："我们今天所做的事，是为明天做准备；今年所做的事，是为明年做准备；今生所做的事，是为来生做准备；生生世世所做的事，是为成佛做准备。现在还不是最好，唯有成佛才是最好！"

II. Chairing Academies

i. Buddhist Academy of Fujian Province

Buddhist Academy of Fujian Province was established by Ven. Master Yuanzhuo and others on April 1st, 1983 with the approval of the Government of Fujian Province and the State Administration for Religious Affairs. It is a Buddhist academy at the provincial level and one of the earliest Buddhist academies established since the reform and opening up of China. The Academy consists of Male Division located at Putian Guanghua Monastery and Female Division at Chongfu Monastery of Fuzhou, which is renowned as the leading nunnery south of the Yangtze River.

▶ 2010 年 9 月 28 日 与福建佛学院 2010 级学僧合影
A group photo with the monastics of Grade 2010, Buddhist Academy of Fujian Province. September 28th, 2010

二、主持学院

1. 福建佛学院

福建佛学院是于 1983 年 4 月 1 日由当代高僧圆拙老和尚等发起、经福建省人民政府与国家宗教事务局批准成立的，属于省级佛教院校，是中国改革开放以来创办较早的佛教院校。学院分男众、女众两部，男众部设在莆田广化寺内，女众部设在享有"江南第一女众丛林"美誉的福州崇福寺内。

▶ 福建佛学院（男众部）
Buddhist Academy of Fujian Province (Male Division)

As President of the Academy, Master Xuecheng serves as a link between the past and future. Rev. Zhao Puchu, pointed out that the cultivation of monastics should always be the top priority of Buddhism at present and for a long time to come. Guided by this, Master has accumulated many years of experience in study and practice and has also observed the learning system of leading domestic and international monasteries. Given the fact that modern monastic practices are vastly different from the ancient reclusive monastic practices, Master advocates integrating three language families of Buddhism and promoting all eight sects of Han Buddhism. With such a vision, Master has brought forward and implemented the idea of Four Becomings: "the monastery becoming academic, the academy becoming monastic, the learning and practice becoming integrated, and the management becoming scientific." The Academy takes the four Bodhisattva qualities of "compassion, wisdom, aspiration and action" as its motto and aims to cultivate modern monastics who excel in "aspiration, cultivation, ability, merit and knowledge" under the ten practice principles: honoring the Three Jewels, respecting teachers and their teachings, restraining the six sensory faculties, eliminating bad habits, developing faith, establishing right views, accumulating merits through hard-working, coordinating understanding with practicing and being pure and harmonious.

Keeping in mind Rev. Zhao Puchu's teaching, that is, the cultivation of monastics should be the top priority of Buddhism at present, Master has been committed to cultivating the Sangha for years. Master said, "Chinese Buddhism lacks excellent Sangha members, therefore their cultivation is urgent. Only persistent efforts for ten or even twenty years can have some effects." From 1990 to 1994, when the Teaching Affairs Office was in crisis due to lack of teachers, he taught 16 classes per week. He vowed, "Even if there is only one student monk left, the Buddhist Academy shall not stop functioning." Master always taught through example. He led the teachers and students of the Academy in morning and evening recitations, eating meals together at the refectory, doing labor work, keeping the Uposatha tradition of chanting precepts, engaging in summer retreats, practicing Buddha name chanting and meditating. These activities are carried out in accordance with the Teachings and Vinaya, thus creating an environment that integrates learning with practice and equally emphasizes the understanding and practice of the Teachings.

身为院长的学诚法师承前启后，在赵朴老提出"当前与今后相当时期内佛教最重要的工作：第一是培养人才，第二是培养人才，第三还是培养人才"的目标引导下，根据多年的修学体悟以及观摩国内外各大道场办学方式的经验，针对现代丛林修行方式不同于古代隐居丛林这一实际状况，以三大语系并融、八大宗派并弘的胸怀，前瞻性地提出并实践"丛林学院化，学院丛林化，修学一体化，管理科学化"的"四化"办学理念。学院以"悲、智、愿、行"四大菩萨之精神为院训；以"恭敬三宝、尊师重道、防护六根、修改习气、培养信心、树立正见、刻苦修学、积福耐劳、解行相应、清净和合"十条为修学原则，培养具备"志、道、德、才、学"等素质的现代出家众。

法师牢记赵朴老当前佛教最首要的问题是培养人才之教诲，多年来一直致力于育僧工作。他说："中国佛教僧才缺乏，亟需培养，要十年二十年紧抓不懈地努力，才会有成效。"1990 年至 1994 年间，教务处出现师资危机，法师每周讲 16 节课，并且发愿："只要有一个学僧，也要将佛学院办下去！"平时，法师身体力行，带领全院师生二时课诵、过堂用斋、出坡劳动、布萨诵戒、结夏安居、念佛禅修等，如法如律、井然有序，形成了学修一体、解行并重的修学氛围。

Master is also very concerned about the infrastructure construction of the Buddhist Academy. In early days, the facility was simple and insufficient. Therefore, in 1999 he personally created the designs for and participated in the building of a new classroom complex with a number of new facilities such as audio-visual classrooms, greatly improved the hardware conditions of the Academy. The Academy has had a strong teaching faculty. Masters like Ven. Zhimin, Ven. Jiequan, Ven. Huihai, Ven. Shengyue, Ven. Yanlian, Ven. Miaofeng, Ven. Fakong, Ven. Dayang, Ven. Puti and Ven. Zhenyu have in turn taken charge of the Teaching Affairs Division of the Male's Department. The Venerables responsible for the teaching have included, among others, Ven. Jiqun, Ven. Ruiyin, Ven. Zhaoming, Ven. Xiankong, Ven. Fahui, Ven. Jixiang, Ven. Yanwu, Ven. Bozhou and Ven. Zhengcan.

▶ 2000 年 5 月　与日常老和尚在福建佛学院
With Ven. Master Richang at Buddhist Academy of Fujian Province. May 2000

　　法师还十分关心佛学院的基础设施建设。学院早期的办学条件相对简陋，1999年，法师亲自设计图纸，筹建风格独特的新教学大楼，增设电教室等多项硬件设施，大大改善了办学条件。学院师资力量雄厚，男众部教务工作先后由智敏、界诠、慧海、圣悦、演莲、妙峰、法空、达阳、菩提、振宇等法师负责；教学方面主要有济群、瑞印、照明、贤空、法辉、寂相、演悟、般舟、正参等法师。

▶ 　2001 年 10 月　与日常老和尚在莆田广化寺
　　 With Ven. Master Richang at Putian Guanghua Monastery. October 2001

The achievements of the Academy over the past decade could have not been possible without Master's selfless dedication. In August 2009, due to the effort made by Master, the State Administration for Religious Affairs approved the Academy's request to upgrade its three-year junior college program to a four-year undergraduate program. At present, the Academy offers three-level programs, i.e. the two-year secondary specialized program, the four-year undergraduate program and the three-year advanced study course. There are 150 monastic students, 30 Dharma teachers and 10 guest lecturers at the Academy.

By the end of 2011, Buddhist Academy of Fujian Province had been annually producing graduates for 12 years, giving over 1,400 graduation certificates and certificates of completion. A large number of young monks have emerged with a possession of moral integrity and ability, good character and knowledge. Some of them have committed themselves to teaching, some are engaged in Buddhist research, some are devoted to charity work, some have become abbots, and guiding people in Buddhist cultivation and some others have traveled abroad to promote Dharma. These excellent monks have provided a momentum for Buddhism and have breathed new life into the religion and culture, greatly contributing to the dissemination of Dharma.

Year after year, with his simple style and unshakeable faith, Master has passed this "patriotism to the nation and faithfulness to Buddhism" and lofty ideal of "Honor the land and benefit living beings" to the teachers and students of the Academy. Under his leadership, the Academy is full of vigor and vitality.

　　学院这十几年来所取得的成就与法师多年来无我无私的付出是分不开的。在他的努力下，2009 年 8 月，国家宗教事务局批复了佛学院专科升本科的请示，使佛学院的教育、弘法功能更上一层楼。目前学院设有中专班、本科班、研究班三个梯次，中专班学制两年，本科班学制四年，研究班学制三年。在校学僧 150 名，法师 30 名，外聘教师 10 名。

　　至 2011 年，福建佛学院已有 12 届毕业生，毕业、结业者 1400 多名。一大批德才兼备、品学兼优的青年法师脱颖而出，他们或走上讲坛，或从事佛学研究工作，或开创慈善事业，或住持一方领众熏修，或到海外弘法。这些佛教人才给佛教事业注入了新的生机与活力，为佛法的弘传做出了重要贡献。

　　法师以淳朴的作风和坚定的信念，向一届又一届佛学院师生传递着爱国爱教的思想情操及"庄严国土，利乐有情"的崇高理想。在他的带领下，福建佛学院不断焕发出勃勃生机。

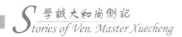
ii. Famen Monastery Buddhist Academy

Since he assumed abbotship of Famen Monastery on January 16th, 2004, to fulfill the wishes of the former Abbot, the late Ven. Master Jingyi, Master has made up his mind to prepare for the establishment of Shaanxi Famen Monastery Buddhist Academy.

▶ 2005 年 5 月 13 日 与法门寺佛学班（法门寺佛学院前身）师生合影
A group photo with the faculty and students of Famen Monastery Buddhist Class (the predecessor of Famen Monastery Buddhist Academy). May 13th, 2005

2. 法门寺佛学院

学诚法师自 2004 年 1 月 16 日担任法门寺住持后，秉承着前任方丈净一老和尚的遗愿，开始发心筹建陕西法门寺佛学院。

▶ 法门寺佛学院
Famen Monastery Buddhist Academy

Under Master's elaborate planning and guidance, Famen Monastery Buddhist Class was established on November 11th, 2004, the birthday of Medicine Buddha. With Master's persistent efforts for three years, Famen Monastery Buddhist Class, which started from nothing, developed into large, regular classes. Its software and hardware facilities matched those of an intermediate and advanced academy. In December 2007, with approval from the State Administration for Religious Affairs, Famen Monastery Buddhist Academy started to run on a trial basis. In May 2010, Famen Monastery Buddhist Academy was officially established as a Buddhist academy at provincial level, the first Han Buddhist academy in Northwest China, located inside Famen Monastery.

The facilities of the Academy were prepared and built under the resolution of the late Abbot Ven. Jingyi, between 1997 and 2002. Currently, there are 8 classroom buildings, 4 large classrooms, 1 lecture hall and 1 library. Each building is equipped with a heating system and teaching facilities such as projectors and computers. The audio-visual classroom and the stadium are under construction. The facilities can accommodate 300 students. The library has a collection of nearly 10,000 books, five sets of Tripitakas and dozens of different Buddhist magazines, which meet the basic requirements of teaching and learning at present.

The Academy and Buddhist Academy of Fujian Province share the same educational concepts. In the summer of 2006, in order to strengthen the communication and cooperation between Famen Monastery Buddhist Class and Buddhist Academy of Fujian Province, Master instructed that a class from each institute should attend the other's summer retreat so that they may learn from each other. This produced remarkable results.

Attracted by Master's compassion and vows, a number of high quality teaching and administrative faculty from around China came to Famen Monastery Buddhist Academy, including those from Buddhist Academy of China, Buddhist Academy of Fujian Province, etc. The faculty keeps stable, consisting of teachers who teach in an earnest and responsible spirit and manage by setting up models themselves. The Dharma teachers have strong determination for cultivation and pious faith. Besides running the Academy, they take an active part in the important receptions and Dharma assemblies of Famen Monastery. At

2004 年 11 月 11 日，适逢药师佛圣诞，在法师的精心策划与指导下，法门寺佛学班在这个吉祥的日子成立了。经过法师三年多矢志不渝的努力与推动，法门寺佛学班从无到有，从小到大，从不正规渐渐走向正规，佛学班的软件、硬件设施已经达到中上级佛学院的水平。因缘聚会，2007 年 12 月，法门寺佛学院经国家宗教事务局批准，开始试运行。2010 年 5 月，法门寺佛学院正式成立，属于省级佛教院校。学院位于陕西法门寺院内，是西北第一所汉传高等佛学院。

佛学院硬件设施，由已故前任方丈净一老和尚于 1997 年至 2002 年发大心筹建。目前有教学楼八栋、大教室四个、大讲堂一座和图书馆一座，每栋楼都安装了暖气设备；佛学院配备了投影仪、计算机等现代化教学器材；电教室和体育场正在筹建中。硬件设备可以招收 300 名学生。图书馆藏书近万册，其中藏经五部，各类佛教杂志数十种，基本能满足目前教学的需要。

学院与福建佛学院的办学理念一脉相承。早在 2006 年夏，法师为了加强法门寺佛学班与福建佛学院的交流与合作，利用结夏安居的三个月时间，让彼此互派一个班参加对方寺院的结夏安居，相互观摩与学习，效果显著。

在法师悲心愿力的感召下，很快从四面八方涌来一批高素质的教职人才。他们分别来自中国佛学院、福建佛学院等，教师队伍稳定，教学认真负责，管理以身作则。法师们道心坚固、信仰虔诚，除了佛学院的工作之外，还积极参与承担法门寺的重大接待和重大

the opening of the Academy, there were only 24 students, but one year later its distinctions and advantages won increasing recognition from both within and out of Buddhist society. There were 92 students in three classes: a secondary specialized class, a junior college class and an undergraduate class.

On July 24th, 2009, Famen Monastery Buddhist Academy held a graduation ceremony for its first graduates. Despite his tight schedule, Master Xuecheng, as Abbot of Famen Monastery and President of Famen Monastery Buddhist Academy, came from Beijing to attend the graduation ceremony. He addressed the graduates, "Be modest, try to let go of oneself, let go of self attachment, and be obedient to living beings. Do things in accordance with the Middle Way principle, do things appropriately, deal with every kind of relationship skillfully with Dharma wisdom and do one's own job well. Take initiative to practice and promote Dharma, and make great resolve to undertake the responsibilities of disseminating Dharma and benefiting living beings."

By 2011, Famen Monastery Buddhist Academy had produced graduates for two consecutive years. More than 100 graduation certificates and certificates of completion were awarded. At present, the Academy offers two-levels of programs: a four-year undergraduate program and a three-year postgraduate program. Currently there are 60 monastic students, 20 Dharma teachers and 7 guest lecturers. These achievements were made impossible without Master's efforts. With Master's leadership, Famen Monastery Buddhist Academy will witness a brighter future.

法会的工作。学院成立伊始，只有 24 位同学，经过一年的教学实践，佛学院的办学特点和优势得到教内外的认可，发展到三个班级，共 92 人，分别为中专班、大专班和本科班。

2009 年 7 月 24 日，法门寺佛学院迎来了首届毕业生举行毕业典礼的日子。作为法门寺佛学院院长、法门寺住持的学诚法师，在法务十分繁忙的情况下，特地从北京赶来参加学僧们的毕业典礼。法师在典礼上开示道："做人要谦虚，要努力地放下自我，放下我执，随顺众生；做事要遵循中道的原则，做事要恰到好处，通过佛法的智慧，方便善巧地处理各种关系，做好自己承担的相应职位的工作；修行、弘法要积极，要发大愿心，承担起弘扬正法、利益众生的责任。"

至 2011 年，法门寺佛学院已有两届毕业生，毕业、结业者 100 多名。学院目前设有本科班、研究班两个梯次，本科班学制四年，研究班三年，在校学僧 60 名，执教法师 20 名，外聘教师 7 名。学院这几年来所取得的成就与法师的付出是分不开的，在他的带领下，法门寺佛学院一定会有更加美好的前景。

Chapter Six

Promoting Dharma Extensively, Keeping Pace with the Times

■ Master Xuecheng perceptively takes hold of the conditions of today's world to develop a profound insight on the relationship between promoting traditional Chinese culture and revitalizing Buddha's Teachings. As a religious leader, with a broad mind and far-reaching vision not limited to one single religion or sect, Master has suggested to establish a platform for advocating traditional Chinese culture, whose values could provide good solutions to various problems of today's society.

■ With conditions becoming favorable, Master started to give speeches and disseminate the Dharma to the general public. Those lectures include "Strengthening the Development of National Culture as a Soft Power", "Cultural Soft Power and Buddhist Culture", "The Universal Value of Buddhist Culture" and "The Modern Significance of Buddhist Culture".

第六章

广弘佛法　与时俱进

■　学诚法师敏锐地把握了当前时空因缘，深入地思考和抉择了弘扬传统文化与振兴佛法之间的关系，以一个宗教界领袖宽广的心胸和高远的格局，超越宗派、宗教，倡议搭建一个传播中华传统文化的平台，用中国传统文化价值观来解读当今社会所存在的诸多问题。

■　法师随顺因缘开始步入社会演讲、弘法，陆续做了《加强国家文化软实力建设》《文化软实力与佛教文化》《佛教文化的普世价值》《佛教文化的现代意义》等报告和讲座。

Master believes that Buddhist education should guide the fourfold assembly of disciples to free themselves from primitive, unilateral, backward, short-sighted and outdated thinking, and take a path that leads toward society and the whole world. On one hand, Buddhists should focus on self-cultivation: inspiring others with Dharma, gaining the support of others by virtue, benefiting oneself and others, enlightening oneself and others and engaging oneself with true practice and the true promotion of the Teachings. On the other hand, they must understand the development of Buddhism in this new era, not just focus on the current situation and must learn how to use modern technologies like computers and the Internet. They must make use of methods that are suitable to the lifestyle of people in modern times so as to disseminate the Dharma.

In 2006, time came for Master to use the Internet to promote Buddhism. While on a flight, a friend of Master offered to help him set up a blog. Master accepted it and started the blog on February 21st. Since the blog was launched, Master has posted many entries about how he leads his disciples to integrate the Teachings into real life, modernizing Buddhism. It has received universal acclaim among media, devotees and the general public.

Xu Chang'an, a journalist from China News Agency, once reported in 2006, "Blogs have not been popular in China for very long, but they have extensively attracted netizens, including Chinese Buddhists. Ven. Master Xuecheng, Vice President of Buddhist Association of China showed great interest in blogging, making him 'the first Buddhist monk in China to have a blog'. Master Xuecheng communicates with his students via the blog, as if he were teaching in a real classroom. It has benefited both the teacher and the students. Master's blog has stories about his participation in different events, for example, his speech at the First World Buddhist Forum. There are also Q&A records between him and netizens. The following example clearly indicates the monastic role the blog serves. In August this year, a netizen named Jueyuan posted a question on the blog. He said, 'Venerable Master, I feel that recently I have remained stagnant in my practice. I have failed to get rid of bad habits. I have been chanting Buddha's name and the mantra as usual, but for the past few years I've always felt that I have made little progress. It seems I have reached a bottle-neck and cannot move forward. How can I overcome it?' Master replied, 'There are three criteria that you can use to check whether you have made progress in practice: having subdued afflictions or not; having cultivated firm belief in the law of causality or not; and having followed precepts strictly or not.'"

法师认为，佛教的教育应该引导四众弟子从原始、片面、落后、短视、陈旧的观念里解放出来，走面向社会、面向世界的道路。除了要注重自身修养——以道感人、以德服人、自利利他、自觉觉他、真实修行、真实弘法之外，作为佛教徒，还要有长远的眼光，要能够把握新时代佛教发展的命脉，要懂得利用现代科技（如电脑、网络等）和适合现代人生活方式的方法来弘法。

2006 年，开展网络弘法的机缘日臻成熟。法师的一位友人在飞机上主动提议为法师开通博客，法师随顺因缘，于 2 月 21 日开始启用。博客开通以后，一幅幅由法师带领弟子们将佛法生活化、现代化的鲜活画面源源不断地透过互联网展现出来，赢得了媒体、广大信众和普通民众的一致好评。

中新社记者徐长安在 2006 年曾这样报道："博客 (Blog) 在中国兴起尚无多少时日，在迅即引起广大网民参与之时，也引起中国佛教界人士的兴趣。中国佛教协会副会长学诚大和尚对博客的热衷，使他成为中国佛教界'博客第一人'。自从开了博客，学诚就像为自己开了一个课堂一样，通过博客和学生交流，师生相得益彰。其中既有关于自己参加活动的报道，例如今年首届世界佛教论坛期间学诚的演讲，也有他和网友的问答。举一个例子便可窥见学诚博客道场之一斑。今年 8 月，一位叫觉缘的网友留言：'师父：弟子最近修行总是不进不退，该改掉的习气，也一直没能改掉。我也如常，念佛念咒。这些年来总觉得自己没能进步，一直卡在某个关口，无法前进。弟子该如何突破？'学诚回复：'检验修行是否进步有三个标准：烦恼调伏否？业果深信否？戒律清净否？'"

Master talked about the reasons for launching his blog and his opinions about it on Phoenix TV, Hong Kong, in a dialogue session during the 2nd World Buddhist Forum in 2009. He said, "In 2006 one of my friends set up a blog for me on sina.com and then came to the Monastery to give it to me. At that time I had no idea what a blog was, but he convinced me to give it a try. I thought that because he had already set it up, there might be some negative effects if I closed it. Thus I started working on it."

▶ 2009 年 12 月 4 日 在北京龙泉寺见行堂看博客
Reviewing the blog, Jianxing Hall, Beijing Longquan Monastery. December 4th, 2009

"At the beginning, I asked myself how I should proceed. I posted some articles I had previously published. After I had posted them all, I wondered what else I could do. Later I took a survey and found that people are quite interested in how we monks study, practice and cultivate at monasteries. People want to know about what kind of life we live. Since then, the monks at our monastery have been working together on the blog."

　　法师在 2009 年第二届世界佛教论坛的一次座谈中，面对香港凤凰卫视，叙述了他开博客的因缘和想法："2006 年的时候，我的一个朋友，在新浪网上面给我开了一个博客，送到庙里面来。起初我还不明白这个博客是什么意思，然后他就跟我讲，你不妨试试看。我后来想，他已经开好了，要把它关掉的话，到时候这个影响也不好，所以就接着做。"

▶　法师的龙泉之声博客
Master's blog on Voice of Longquan

　　"刚刚开始的时候，我想，怎么做呢？我就把过去自己发表的一些文章拿到上面去登。登完了没有东西登，那怎么办呢？后来我就去做了一个调查。大家说，非常喜欢了解寺庙里面的出家人是怎么学习、怎么修行、怎么用功的，他们是过着怎么样的一种生活，之后我们庙里面的这些法师们就一起进行集体创作。"

"My blog is more than a personal one, it's a blog of many. We write articles and post them on the blog. Once they are posted, many Buddhists, as well as the believers of other religions and non-believers, read them and post their comments. Then I reply to and answer what they have asked. My principle is that as long as you make comments or ask questions, I will respond. Through this process, I have come to realize that to promote Dharma, we must employ modern media and modern communication methods. However large our monastery may be, it's still very difficult for people to come a long way to the monastery to meet a monk. If one lives in Shanghai, or much farther like in Guangzhou, Taiwan, or even the United States or Japan, he or she has to spend a lot of money on airfare as well as a lot of time to come here. With a blog, this problem does not exist. We can post our Dharma lectures in either audio or video format, and can answer questions too. In this way, our thoughts and the Dharma we should preach can all be conveyed to Buddhists and the whole society. I believe that if it were possible, Ven. Master Xuanzang, Ven. Master Kumarajiva and Ven. Master Jianzhen would have set up blogs in their times."

By January 26th, 2012, it had more than 8.6 million visits, attracting a large number of netizens to study Dharma and serving as a platform for Master to communicate and interact with devotees and people from all walks of life.

After sina.com introduced the function of uploading videos, in March 2009, Master added a video broadcast to the Blog which distributes the Dharma talks, monastic events, and so on.

Master perceptively takes hold of the conditions of today's world to develop a profound insight on the relationship between promoting traditional Chinese culture and revitalizing Buddha's Teachings. As a religious leader, with a broad mind and far-reaching vision not limited to one single religion or sect, Master has suggested to establish a platform for advocating traditional Chinese culture, whose values could provide good solutions to various problems of today's society. This is an action to share the concerns of our nation and reinforce the competitiveness of Chinese nationality. By doing so, Buddhism will also be able to take root in an extended area. Therefore, it

"所以我这个博客，不仅仅是一个个人的博客，还是一个众人的博客，大家一起写文章到上面去发表。发表了以后呢，吸引了很多的佛教信徒，也包括其他一些宗教的信徒，当然也有不少没有宗教信仰的人，在上面留言。那么留言就要回复，有问必答，我是这样的一个原则，只要你留言，肯定都会有回答。那么，在这样一个过程当中，我就慢慢体会到，佛教要弘法，需要利用现代传媒的方法，利用现代化的手段。不然的话，我们庙里边即使修得再大，他从很远的地方跑到庙里面来见一个出家的法师也是非常不容易的。比如说他在上海要跑到北京很不容易，在广州，在台湾，甚至在美国、日本，那你要花费很多的机票钱，同时也会浪费时间。但是在博客上面就不存在这个问题，我们讲经说法的一些视频、音频，以及一些问答，都可以在上面发布。这样的话，我们的一些思想，我们自己要讲的佛法，都可以很好地同信教群众以及社会各界正面进行交流。那么我想，如果是在古代的时候，玄奘大师也好，鸠摩罗什大师也好，鉴真大师也好，他们也会开博客的。"

从博客开通至 2012 年 1 月 26 日，点击量已超过 860 万人次，接引了大批网友学习佛法，成为法师与广大信教群众和社会各界人士交流互动的一个很好的平台。

随着新浪网开通上传视频的功能，法师于 2009 年 3 月开通播客，将弘法开示和寺院活动等视频发布到网上。

法师敏锐地把握了当前时空因缘，深入地思考和抉择了弘扬传统文化与振兴佛法之间的关系，以一个宗教界领袖宽广的心胸和高远的格局，超越宗派、宗教，倡议搭建一个传播中华传统文化的平台，用中国传统文化价值观来解读当今社会所存在的诸多问题，既

facilitates a wonderful combination between patriotism and religious faith, doctrinally reasonable and factually feasible.

From this high standpoint, Master directed the establishing of Voice of Longquan website, which was officially launched at 8:08:08 a.m., August 8th, 2008. At the opening ceremony, Master said, "We have set up the Voice of Longquan website to allow traditional Chinese culture to meet people's needs, to keep pace with the times and to help live up to the fundamental mission of Buddhism. We hope that in the future more and more people will visit and support our website. We hope that it will act as a successful tool for disseminating Dharma, benefiting living beings, promoting traditional Chinese culture and allowing us to communicate with each other and learn the latest news about Buddhism and other religions. Let's make a concerted effort to lead Buddhism onto a track of healthy development. May our bliss and wisdom grow day by day. Today is a new beginning. We will work hard together. Best wishes to you all."

With Buddhism as the core and Confucianism and Taoism as two wings, Voice of Longquan website advocates the thoughts of traditional Chinese culture featured with humanity and harmony, and spreads them throughout the world. The Chinese website comprises channels of Longquan Monastery, Multi-culture, Man and Society, Man and Nature, Cultivation of Mind, Taste of Life, Celebrities' Column, Special Features, etc. Other channels launched at a later time include Master's Blog, E-Paper, Video Station, Longquan Forum, etc. The website allows netizens to learn about traditional Chinese culture. Also, the first foreign language (English) version of the website was launched on the day of the closing ceremony of the Beijing Olympics (August 24th, 2008), as an effort of international outreach. Regarding the influence of the website, it received 419,261 clicks and 70,318 visits only four months after its launching. These hits were made by 23,083 visitors from 555 cities in 45 countries around the globe. On February 17th, 2011, the Japanese version of Voice of Longquan was launched. It is expected that in the future, other versions will be launched in languages such as Korean, French etc. This is to facilitate the exchanges between the East and the West, and to promote traditional Chinese culture and its values. Up to January 26th, 2012, the page view count of the Voice of Longquan has reached more than 11 million hits.

是为国分忧，增强中华民族的竞争力，又使佛法得以扎根于一个广大的平台上，将爱国与爱教契理契机地结合在一起。

正是站在这样一个至高的着眼点上，在法师的指导下，2008 年 8 月 8 日上午 8 时 8 分 8 秒，龙泉之声网站正式开通。在网站开通仪式上，法师说："我们做龙泉之声网站，其目的就是要符合传统文化，符合大众的需要，符合时代的发展，符合佛教根本宗旨。今后我们还是希望更多的人关注、参与、支持，把这个网站能够办成弘法利生的平台，办成传播弘扬传统文化的平台，办成一个我们互相交流的平台，办成我们了解各种时代最新佛教和宗教信息的平台。让我们佛教越来越朝着健康的轨道发展，让我们自己的福德智慧资粮一天又一天不断地增长，今天是个新的起点，今后大家要共同努力。祝福大家！"

龙泉之声网站以佛法为核心，儒、道为两翼，弘扬中华传统文化中的"人本""和谐"的思想，并使之放声于世界。网站设立龙泉道场、多元文化、人与社会、人与自然、修心养性、品味生活、名家专栏、专题等中文频道，后来又陆续增加了法师博客、电子报、视频网、龙泉论坛等频道。为广大网友提供了一个了解、学习传统文化的平台。为了使网站更具有国际影响力，2008 年 8 月 24 日，北京奥运会闭幕当天，龙泉之声网站第一个外语（英语）频道开通。网站运行仅四个月，便接受了 419,261 次点击，70,318 次访问，更有来自于全球 45 个国家 555 个城市的 23,083 名唯一访问者。2011 年 2 月 17 日，龙泉之声日文版开通，未来更期望开通韩、法等多语种频道，以更好地促进东西方文化交流，宣扬中华传统文化及其价值观。至 2012 年 1 月 26 日，龙泉之声网站的浏览量已超过 1,100 万次。

On April 11th, 2009, Master Xuecheng's Twitter, another platform for promoting Buddhism was established (Chinese: http://zuosa.com/xuechengfashi, English: http://twitter.com/xuecheng). The use of micro-blogging holds great significance, showing that Buddhism keeps pace with trends and has many expedient ways to disseminate Dharma. Master said, "In terms of promoting Dharma, Buddhism should keep pace with the times. It is essential for Buddhism to exist in forms that are easy for people to access. Therefore, we should always promote new methods of communication, cultivating innovation." One of Master's disciples said, "Our teacher is following the trends by using microblogs." Master answered, "No, leading the trend." Other websites that Longquan Monastery has launched later are Voice of Longquan microblog (http://www.longquanzs.org/t/), Digu microblog (http://digu.com/xuecheng), Tongxue microblog (http://tongxue.com/shixuecheng) and Sina microblog (http://weibo.com/xuecheng).

Master launched his multilingual microblogs on February 17th (the fifteenth day of the first month of the lunar calendar), 2011. On the websites of qq.com, sina.com and bentio.com, microblogs are set up in 8 languages i.e. Chinese, English, French, German, Russian, Japanese, Korean and Spanish. The Chinese ones are put on http://t.qq.com/xuechengfashi, http://weibo.com/xuecheng and http://bentio.com/xuechengfashigb, where readers can follow the links to other language editions. More microblogs of Master have been established in Japan, Korea and Russia, including http://now.ameba.jp/xuechengfashi (Japanese), http://me2day.net/shixuecheng (Korean) and http://www.rutwit.ru/xuechengfashi (Russian).

Master's microblogs are updated daily in 8 different languages, taking a significant step in the international promotion of Dharma. Master's launching of the multilingual microblogs has been reported through dozens of media outlets such as people.com.cn, xinhuanet.com, ifeng.com, chinanews.com, cnr.cn, *China Youth Daily*, *China Culture Report*, *Beijing Evening News*, *Global Times* (overseas edition), BBC and CNN, etc. "Such an accomplishment is definitely the first in China and is still rare in the rest of the world", remarked people.com.cn. Master's

2009 年 4 月 11 日，法师又建立了一个全新的弘法平台——学诚法师微博（中文站点 http://zuosa.com/xuechengfashi，英文站点 http://twitter.com/xuecheng）。学诚法师微博的推出具有划时代的意义，向世人昭示着佛法并不落伍，佛法弘扬是善巧方便的，是能够把握时代脉搏的。学诚法师说："佛教的发展在弘法的方式、方法上也应恰当地与时俱进。在这个时空因缘下，就必须要以民众容易接受的形式存在，我们要有越来越多的方法，要不断去创新，不断有新方式出现。"学诚法师的弟子说："师父开微博也赶潮流了。"法师说："是引领潮流。"随后开通的站点有：龙泉之声微博 http://www.longquanzs.org/t/，嘀咕微博 http://digu.com/xuecheng，同学网 http://tongxue.com/shixuecheng，新浪微博 http://weibo.com/xuecheng。

2011 年 2 月 17 日（农历正月十五），法师又开通了多语种微博。在国内的腾讯和新浪网站及国外 www.bentio.com 网站上分别开通了中、英、法、德、俄、日、韩、西班牙语八个语种的微博，其中中文微博网址分别为：http://weibo.com/xuecheng，http://weibo.com/xuecheng 和 http://bentio.com/xuechengfashigb，由中文微博页面可以访问到其他语种的站点。另外在日本、韩国和俄罗斯的网站上也分别开设了日语 http://now.ameba.jp/xuechengfashi、韩语 http://me2day.net/shixuecheng 及俄语 http://www.rutwit.ru/xuechengfashi 的微博。

法师的微博每天用八种语言更新，为国际化弘法迈出了关键性的一步。人民网、新华网、凤凰网、中国新闻网、中国广播网、《中国青年报》《中国文化报》《北京晚报》《环球时报（海外版）》BBC、CNN 等国内外十余家媒体对法师的多语种微博进行了报道。人民网评价法师的多语种微博不仅在国内首创，在国际上也是罕见

multilingual microblogs are a reflection of his deep devotion and timely mastery of current causes and conditions. By January 26th, 2012, more than 200,000 people in total had become fans of Master's microblogs.

On July 28th, 2011, advancing with the times, Master launched Qing-blog in addition to his blog and microblog accounts. In order to spread Dharma in modern society, Master initiated a cartoon series in Qing-blog, introducing the monks and lay people's lives at Longquan Monastery. The cartoon was created to help people learn about and understand Buddhist Dharma in an easy and relaxing way, so that Buddhist culture could be integrated into people's minds.

▶ 法师的轻博客 漫画系列
Cartoon series of Master's Qing-blog

的。多语种微博的开通体现了学诚法师深切的愿力和对现有时代因缘的把握。截止到 2012 年 1 月 26 日，法师多语种微博的"粉丝"数量合计已经突破 20 万人。

2011 年 7 月 28 日，法师与时俱进，继博客、微博后又开通了轻博客，这是目前最新最时尚的网络平台。为适应现代弘法的需要，法师开始推出漫画系列，以漫画的形式表现龙泉寺僧俗二众的学修生活，使大众通过喜闻乐见的形式认识和了解佛法，让佛教文化的涓涓清流汇入茫茫的人海思潮。

In his article "Self-Cultivation and the Spreading of Buddhism under Conditions of Space and Time", Master said, "China has a population exceeding one billion, therefore, we must employ modern technologies to extensively benefit all living beings. Merely relying on traditional forms of communication is no longer sufficient. In this age of information, we should spread Dharma speedily with the help of information technology so that people from all walks of life are able to have access to the voice of the Dharma. Traditional means can hardly offer the same chances of learning Buddha's Teachings as the Internet, which makes promoting Buddhism easy and convenient, regardless of distance. These are the characteristics of this generation. Only when we have a comprehensive understanding of our times, can we do things in a proper way. The agricultural era relies on farming, and farming relies on manual labor. Therefore, many hands make light work. The industrial age relies on machines and science, therefore the more advanced the machines are, the better success there will be. In this post-industrial era, information is valued. If you have a piece of information, you can only succeed when you spread it and make people understand and accept it."

"This is an Internet age. The development of each industry depends on the Internet. Everything is connected to each other in the same way as Internet links up different items totally. Isolation is equivalent to weakness. That's why all industries and organizations rely heavily on the Internet, which shows the strength of collective karma. Being connected as one is collective karma. We will be weak if what we Buddhists do only creates individual karma. If we are weak, we are unable to influence society extensively."

Master complies with specific causes and conditions, and is able to seize opportunities. Master said, "I do not have fixed ideas while doing things. I only possess absolute faith in the Buddha Dharma. Other things can be adjusted according to circumstances."

With favorable causes and conditions, Master started to give speeches and disseminate the Dharma to the general public. On April 21st, 2007, he delivered a lecture entitled "Faith and Life" at Peking University for participants of the "High-level Forum for the Growth of Entrepreneurs". He said in his speech, "Today I'll focus on four points. First, the relation between religious faith and social conditions, second, some characteristics of Buddhist faith, third, the understanding of life and concern for life from the Buddhist perspective, and fourth, the fact that Buddhism teaches people to explore the issue of happiness and sufferings of our body and mind."

学诚法师在《时空因缘与内修外弘》一文中说："中国有十几亿人口，要广度众生，就要利用高科技，单靠人力是不够的。现在是信息时代，就要借助信息技术快速地把佛法传播出去，让各阶层的人们都能够听到正法之音。用传统的办法，他们是很难接触到佛法的，可是使用网络传播，就能做到方便快捷、无远弗届。这个时代的特点就是这样，对整个时代的因缘了解了，事情才能做好。农业时代靠农耕，农耕的时候靠人力，人多好办事，人多田很快就种完了；工业化时代靠机器，讲科学，机器越先进干得越好；后工业化时代讲究信息，你有一个信息，怎样把它传播出去，让大家知道、接受，这样才能成功。"

"现在这个时代是网络的时代，各行各业的发展都要网络化，所有的一切都要像网络一样联成一体，孤立肯定没有力量。社会上不管哪一个行业、团体都很强调这一点，这其实就是共业的力量，联成一体就变成共业。如果我们佛教徒所做的都是各个不同的别业，那力量就弱，就没有办法去广泛地影响社会。"

法师顺应因缘、把握机遇、不拘一格。他说："我做事没有绝对固定的想法，只是对佛法有绝对的信心，其他看情况调整。"

法师随顺因缘开始步入社会演讲、弘法。2007 年 4 月 21 日，学诚法师在北京大学为企业家成长高层论坛的学员做《信仰与人生》的专题讲座。在讲座中，他说："我今天讲座分四个部分：第一个部分，宗教信仰与社会因缘；第二个部分，佛教信仰的一些特点；第三个部分，佛教对生命的认识和关怀；第四个部分，佛教教导人们深入认识身心的苦乐。"

On March 9th, 2008, Master gave a speech entitled "Strengthening the Development of National Culture as a Soft Power" at the 3rd session of the 11th National Committee of CPPCC. He said, "The building of Chinese soft power will never attack, dissolve or erode the cultural values of other civilizations, therefore it will never pose a threat to the cultural values of other civilizations. It endeavors to demonstrate the immortal wisdom in its civilization which represents the universal values. It also acknowledges that the same or similar immortal wisdom exists in other civilizations as well. Meanwhile, it also appreciates and respects the uniqueness of other different civilizations. Exclusiveness, homogeneity, domination and expansionism do not correspond with the internal logic of the Chinese civilization. Therefore, cultural hegemony, cultural imperialism and cultural colonialism do not fit into Chinese civilization. Its major attribute is harmony."

On November 21st, 2008, Master gave a speech at Peking University entitled "Cultural Soft Power and Buddhist Culture". About 500 people attended the lecture, including faculty and students of Peking University and lay Buddhists. Master elaborated on Buddhist culture, its relationship to the soft power of Chinese culture and their present and future issues.

On December 11th, 2008, Master was invited by the Institute for the Study of Buddhism and Religious Theory of Renmin University of China to give a lecture entitled "The Universal Value of Buddhist Culture". About 500 people attended the lecture, including Prof. Zhang Fenglei, Prof. Fang Litian, Prof. Zhang Wenliang, Prof. Wen Jinyu, monastics, lay Buddhists, and students from different universities. In his speech, Master explained how to realize the universal values, how to dispel the public's mysterious impression about Buddhism, how to clear up superstition, what true and complete Dharma is, the relationship and differences between Buddhism and science, what is the Buddha's Teaching on Dependent Arising, what are religious lineages about, etc. Master also expressed his insights on Buddha's Teachings and sutras.

2008 年 3 月 9 日，法师在全国政协十一届一次会议第三次全体会议上做了《加强国家文化软实力建设》的大会发言。法师说："中国的软实力建设绝不以自己的文化价值观冲击、消解、侵蚀其他文明的文化价值观，因而绝不会构成对其他文明的文化价值观的威胁，它努力展示自己文明中具有普世价值的不朽智慧，也承认其他文明中也具有相同或相似的不朽智慧，同时欣赏和尊重其他文明中与自己文明不同的特殊所在。单一性、同质性、宰制性、扩张性不符合中华文明的内在逻辑，文化霸权主义、文化帝国主义、文化殖民主义在以和谐为主要特征的中华文明中没有存在的土壤。"

2008 年 11 月 21 日，法师在北京大学做了题为《文化软实力与佛教文化》的演讲，北大师生、佛教居士约 500 人聆听了演讲。法师就佛教文化与当今中国文化软实力的营造、现实与未来等问题做了阐释。

2008 年 12 月 11 日，法师应中国人民大学佛教与宗教学理论研究所的邀请，在人民大学做了《佛教文化的普世价值》专题讲座。人民大学的张风雷、方立天、张文良、温金玉等教授，僧众及居士，各高校的学生近 500 人聆听了讲座。法师就如何实现普世价值，如何摆脱佛教在大众心中的神秘感，如何消除迷信，及什么样的佛法是真正的佛法、圆满的佛法，佛教与科学的区别与联系，佛教缘起法，宗教的传承，以及自己对佛法、经文的体会等方面向听众做了演讲。

```
 1
---+---
 2 | 4
---+
 3
```

▶ 1．2008 年 11 月 21 日 在北京大学做讲座
Giving a lecture at Peking University. November 21st, 2008

▶ 2．2009 年 12 月 12 日 在国家图书馆做讲座
Giving a lecture at the National Library of China. December 12th, 2009

▶ 3．2008 年 12 月 11 日 在中国人民大学做讲座
Giving a lecture at Renmin University of China. December 11th, 2008

▶ 4．2008 年 3 月 9 日 在人民大会堂政协会议上做大会发言
Giving a conference address at CPPCC at the Great Hall of the People. March 9th, 2008

On December 12th, 2009, upon invitation by the National Library, Master gave a lecture there entitled "The Modern Significance of Buddhist Culture". The theme of the speech was interpreted from three aspects: the fundamental connotations of Chinese Buddhist culture, the localization and socialization of Chinese Buddhist culture and the modern significance of Chinese Buddhist culture. Master initiated the concept of "Culture of the Mind" in his lecture. He said, "To seek 'Culture of the Mind' means that we should try to find causes in ourselves and in our minds and create no opposition. A harmonious world begins with our minds. Confronting globalization, the fundamentals of Buddhist culture are human, the mind, and the good and evil in our minds. When we are in a state of purity, harmony, joy, tranquility and serenity, we will find peace and harmony in our minds, our family, our community, our country and the world. In respect of 'Culture of the Mind', Han Buddhism, Tibetan Buddhism and Theravada Buddhism can learn from each other and complement each other. Buddhists in different countries can communicate and cooperate with each other in the field of spiritual building. Buddhist culture will make considerable contributions to the cultural and ideological progress of modern society."

On July 16th, 2010, Master was invited by the CPPCC Shanghai Committee to give a speech entitled "Trend of Chinese Buddhist Culture from a Global Perspective". More than 500 people, including Feng Guoqin, Chairman of the CPPCC Shanghai Committee, attended the lecture. Master remarked, "Globalization brings unprecedented opportunity as well as unprecedented crises. Buddhism can respond well to many major problems caused by globalization. For example, Buddhism and science can accord with each other and complement one another so as to further harmonious development of both material and spiritual civilization. A harmonious co-existence between man and nature can be achieved by following Buddhist concepts of environmental protection and the Buddhist tradition of following precepts. Buddhism has rich thoughts and a long tradition of peace which can promote the establishment of lasting peace. Buddhism can also strengthen the in-depth exchange between Eastern and Western culture." Master also clarified some common misunderstandings about Buddhism. He specifically explained the meaning and significance of the idea that "Contentment is happiness". He pointed out that Chinese Buddhism has gone through localization and socialization and that along with China's increasing influence in the world, Chinese Buddhism is also reaching out to the world. It will play a unique and positive role in promoting religious reconciliation and world peace.

2009 年 12 月 12 日，应国家图书馆的邀请，法师赴国图做了《佛教文化的现代意义》的主题演讲。演讲从三个方面破题：第一、中国佛教文化的基本内涵；第二、中国佛教文化的本土化与社会化；第三、中国佛教文化的现代意义。法师在讲座中倡导"心文化"的概念，他说："'心文化'要从每个人身上找原因，从心里找原因，不造成对立。和谐世界，从心开始。在全球化面前，佛教文化是以人、以心为本，以内心善恶为本。我们内心清净、内心和乐、内心平安，从个人到家庭、从家庭到社区、从社区到国家、从国家到世界也会祥和。在'心文化'方面，汉传、藏传和南传佛教可以优势互补，互相借鉴。不同国家的佛教在精神领域的建设上，可以交流，互相合作。应该说在思想领域、精神领域，佛教文化在现代社会应该会有比较大的贡献。"

2010 年 7 月 16 日，应上海市政协的邀请，学诚法师做了《全球视野下的中国佛教文化走向》专题报告。上海市政协主席冯国勤等共约 500 人参加。法师说："全球化带来空前便利，也带来空前危机。佛教能良好应对全球化的很多重大问题：如佛教能与科学深层契合、形成互补，达成物质文明和精神文明的和谐发展；佛教的环保理念以及戒律传统使人与自然和谐相处；佛教有着丰富的和平思想和悠久的和平传统，能促进建设持久和平；佛教能促进东西方文化的深层沟通等。"法师澄清了一些对佛教的常见误解，特别讲解了"知足常乐"的内涵和意义，还指出中国佛教经历了本土化、社会化，现在随着中国走向世界，中国佛教正在走向全球化，将在促进宗教和解、世界和平中发挥特殊的积极作用。

On August 10th, 2010, Master was invited by the Graduate School of Chinese Academy of Social Sciences to give a speech entitled "Gather Wisdom to Jointly Build Culture of the Mind". It was said that this was the first time the Graduate School of Chinese Academy of Social Sciences invited a Buddhist monk to give a lecture. Master focused his talk on the major problems of our times, analyzed the causes of these problems from different perspectives and levels and clarified the fact that all problems are caused by our minds. He also expounded on the relationship among Buddhism, philosophy and science, cleared up common misunderstandings and prejudices against Buddhism and stated the current situation of Chinese Buddhism and its achievements. Moreover, he explained the positive effects of Buddhist ideas and values, cultivation systems, traditions and customs on human society. In particular, he explained the benefits brought by Buddha's Teachings like Dependent Arising, Emptiness of Nature and Consciousness-Only to contemporary science and philosophy.

On December 28th, 2010, Master was invited to give an academic report entitled "Social Responsibility of Chinese Buddhist Culture" at the First Humanities and Religion Summit held at Beijing Normal University. Master expounded on three parts: the historic process and social function of Chinese Buddhist culture, the modern social responsibility of Chinese Buddhist culture, and the future social mission of Chinese Buddhist culture.

On May 5th, 2011, Master was invited by the School of Humanities and Social Sciences of the North China Electric Power University to give a lecture on "Buddhism and Culture of the Mind". Master was the first Buddhist monk lecturer that had been invited by the University since its establishment in 1958. In his lecture, Master pointed out, "Buddhism teaches us what we are supposed to do, rather than what we like to do. Buddhism enables one to set up a high-profile life philosophy, gain a general perspective of life and map a blueprint of life. People need to have visions to inspire themselves in pursuit of dreams and goals."

On June 25th, 2011, Master was again requested to deliver a speech entitled "Buddhist Ethics and Social Morality" at Beijing Normal University. Master stressed, "Buddhist ethics imply profound and broad compatibility. Its fundamental teachings are able to cover both material and spirit, the mundane world and beyond. Both eternity and modernity are involved."

2010 年 8 月 10 日，应中国社会科学院研究生院的邀请，学诚法师在该院做了以《凝聚智慧　共建人类心文化》为主题的讲座。据了解，这次讲座是社科院研究生院第一次邀请佛教法师做讲座。法师主要陈述了当今时代人类的重大问题，从不同角度和层次分析，将问题的根源明确汇归于人心，又论述佛学、哲学和科学的关系，指破对佛教的通常误解和偏见，介绍中国佛教的现状和作为，宣明佛教思想观念、修养体系、文化传统等对人类社会的积极作用，特别阐述缘起性空、法相唯识等佛教教理教义对当今科学和哲学的助益价值。

2010 年 12 月 28 日，法师应邀在北京师范大学首届人文宗教高端论坛会上做题为《中国佛教文化的社会责任》的学术报告。法师从三个方面进行了阐释：中国佛教文化的历史进程和社会作用，中国佛教文化现代的社会责任，中国佛教文化未来的社会使命。

2011 年 5 月 5 日，法师应华北电力大学人文与社会科学学院的邀请，做了《佛教与心文化》的讲座。这次讲座是华北电力大学从 1958 年创校以来首次请佛教僧人做讲座。法师说："佛教告诉我们需要做我们应该做的事，而不是做我们想做的事。佛教让人树立高远人生观，就是人的鸟瞰图、人生基本蓝图。要有愿景，才会有理想、目标。"

2011 年 6 月 25 日，法师再次受邀，在北京师范大学做题为《佛教伦理与社会道德》的讲座。法师强调："佛教伦理更有着深广的兼容性，其教义基础能兼容物质和精神、世间和出世间等，其内容兼容永恒性和时代性。"

On September 16th, 2011, Master was invited by the Qixia District Government of Nanjing to deliver a lecture entitled "Views on Happiness in Life" at Nanjing University. More than 1,000 people including government officials, monks, lay Buddhists, businessmen, other guests and staff of the University were present to listen to the compassionate lecture. In the lecture, Master talked about the conditions of happiness, views on happiness in the ancient and present times and views of happiness in Chinese Buddhism. Master analyzed the common problems concerning happiness that entrepreneurs especially would encounter in their life, work and Buddhist faith.

On October 20th, 2011, Master was invited by the Research Institute of Religion and Culture and the Center for Buddhist Education Research at Peking University to give a lecture on "An Overview of Chinese Buddhist Education" at its Centennial Auditorium, a multi-functional hall. Master stated, "Since its spread to China, Buddhism has been integrated with Confucianism and Taoism. It later mingled with contemporary Western culture, making its educational means and content richer and more diverse. It has exerted great influence on both ancient and modern Chinese society. In the future, Buddhism will develop toward socialization and globalization and will have a positive impact on the construction of Chinese culture and world peace."

　　2011 年 9 月 16 日，法师应南京栖霞区政府的邀请，在南京大学做了题为《人生的幸福观》的讲座。当日，政府领导、僧众及居士、客商、工作人员、其他来宾等 1,000 余听众现场聆听了法师的慈悲开示。在讲座中，学诚法师讲述了现今社会的幸福状况和幸福观、中国古代社会的幸福观、中国佛教的幸福观等，尤其针对企业家在生活、工作、佛教信仰中常见的幸福观问题作了辨析。

　　2011 年 10 月 20 日，法师应北京大学宗教文化研究院和佛学教育研究中心的邀请，在北京大学百年讲堂多功能报告厅做了题为《中国佛教教育概观》的主题演讲。法师说："佛教传入中国后，与本土的儒道文化深入融合，又与近现代的西方文化结合，教育内容更加广博，教育方法丰富多彩，对中国古代和近现代社会产生重大影响，未来会朝着社会化、全球化的方向发展，对中国文化建设、世界人类和平将具有积极的意义。"

Chapter Seven

Multilateral Exchanges,
Reaching Out to the World

■ Master Xuecheng believes that the development of Buddhism is closely interrelated with the fate of China. China's development is dependent on the rest of the world, just as other nations depend on China. With China's development, Chinese culture will spread to the world, so will Chinese Buddhism.

■ Master said, "We should regard 'Culture of the Mind' as our guideline and promote the Buddhist approach of mind purification, that is, diligently practice precepts, concentration and wisdom to vanquish greed, hatred and ignorance. In this way, we facilitate the formation of a new human civilization holding the 'Culture of the Mind' as its main principle, which takes root in the mind and is practiced in society."

第七章

多方交流　走向世界

■ 学诚法师认为，佛教的发展与国家的命运息息相关，中国的发展需要世界各国来参与，世界各国也离不开中国。伴随着中国的日益强大，中国文化将走向世界，中国佛教也将走向世界。

■ 法师说："我们应以'心文化'为主导，弘扬佛教'勤修戒定慧，熄灭贪嗔痴'的心灵净化方法，促使源自内心、践于社会，以'心文化'为核心的人类新文明的形成。"

Master has earnestly participated in promoting friendly exchanges among religions and cultures both home and abroad. On behalf of the Chinese Buddhist community, Master has led delegations abroad to visit, observe, give lectures and teach the Dharma on more than one hundred trips. He has left his footprints in many countries and regions, including India, Nepal, Thailand, Sri Lanka, Vietnam, Malaysia, Singapore, Indonesia, the Philippines, Japan, Korea, the United States, Canada, Switzerland, France, Spain, Kazakhstan, Cyprus, Egypt, and China's Hong Kong, Macao, and Taiwan. Master believes that the development of Buddhism is closely interrelated with the fate of China. China's development is dependent on the rest of the world, just as other nations depend on China. With China's development, Chinese culture will spread to the world, so will Chinese Buddhism.

▶ 2008 年 7 月 16 日 在西班牙世界对话大会上与陶兰红衣大主教
Standing with Cardinal Jean-Louis Pierre Tauran at the World Conference on Dialogue, Spain.
July 16th, 2008

在开展国内外各种宗教文化间的交流与对话、友好往来、增进友谊等方面，法师更是身体力行，认真承担。他曾代表中国佛教界率团出访、参观、考察、讲经、弘法百余次，印度、尼泊尔、泰国、斯里兰卡、越南、马来西亚、新加坡、印度尼西亚、菲律宾、日本、韩国、美国、加拿大、瑞士、法国、西班牙、哈萨克斯坦、塞浦路斯、埃及及中国香港、澳门、台湾等国家和地区都留下了法师的足迹。法师认为，佛教的发展与国家的命运息息相关，中国的发展需要世界各国来参与，世界各国也离不开中国。伴随着中国的日益强大，中国文化将走向世界，中国佛教也将走向世界。

▶ 1999 年 10 月 23 日 在第二届两岸禅学研讨会上发言
Giving a speech at the 2nd Cross-Strait Seminar on Chan Studies. October 23rd, 1999

At a cross-strait Buddhism exchange seminar, Master said, "Buddhism is facing the Eastern and Western collisions on science, politics, economics and cultures, etc. Buddhism also confronts the necessity of self-construction. The position of Buddhist education in the 21st Century is an important affair that cannot be ignored by the Buddhist communities. Discussions, studies and exchanges at different facets, levels and forms out of the perspective of cross-strait Buddhist education, will bring positive influence to the development of Buddhism on both sides of the Taiwan Strait. Buddhism will work to bring harmony to society, acting as a catalyst for the purification of people's minds."

In 1991, the 25-year-old Master Xuecheng visited Sri Lanka, Nepal and a few other countries. Initially, many people did not believe that such a young monk could be an "abbot". They were convinced only after a round of "research". During the visit, the President and Prime Minister of Sri Lanka had a cordial meeting with the young Chinese "eminent monk". In November 1994, Master visited Thailand, escorting the Buddha's tooth sharira.

On November 29th, 1995, Master and many Tibetan monks attended the world-renowned stately ceremony at the Jokhang Monastery in Lhasa, Tibet, where the Gold Urn Lot-Drawing Ceremony confirmed the 11th Panchen Erdeni's reincarnation. The CCTV News Broadcast reported this historic event that evening, which caused a sensation among Buddhist communities across the country. Master attended the grand ceremony as one of the ten representatives of the Buddhist communities in China and the only representative of Han Buddhism, becoming the first monk of the Han ethnic group to attend such a ceremony in all of history. In December 2005, on behalf of BAC, Master visited Tibet to attend the 10th anniversary celebration of the enthronement of the 11th Panchen Erdeni. He was the only monastic representative of the Han ethnic group.

In May 2004, Master was invited by the Japanese Arigatou Foundation to lead a Chinese religious delegation to Geneva and attend the 2nd World Forum on "The Global Network of Religions for Children". There he made a keynote speech entitled "Let Different Religions and Denominations Join Hands to Create a Better Tomorrow for Children".

在一次海峡两岸佛教交流会上，法师说："佛教正面临着东西方科学、政治、经济、文化等各个方面的冲撞，同时，也存在着自身建设方面的严峻考验，21世纪佛学教育该如何定位，将是佛教界不容忽视的重要问题。从两岸佛学教育的角度出发，进行多方面、多层次、多形式的探讨、研究与交流，对两岸的佛教发展将起到积极的影响与互动作用，使佛教在未来，真正地成为净化人心、祥和社会的催化剂与再造丸。"

1991年，25岁的学诚法师出访斯里兰卡、尼泊尔等国时，起初众人不相信有这么年轻就当上"方丈"的法师，经过一番"调查"，才证实确有其事。斯里兰卡总统和总理还亲切接见了这位中国年轻的"高僧"。1994年11月，法师随侍佛牙舍利出访泰国。

1995年11月29日，在西藏拉萨大昭寺举行的十一世班禅大师转世灵童金瓶掣签仪式上，法师和众多藏僧一起参与了这个举世瞩目的庄严仪式。当晚中央电视台新闻联播报道了这一历史镜头，在全国佛教界引起轰动。这一次，学诚法师是参加盛典的全国佛教界十位代表之一，也是汉语系佛教唯一的代表，成为有史以来出席这种仪式的首位汉族僧人。2005年12月，法师代表中国佛教协会赴西藏参加十一世班禅大师坐床10周年庆典活动，也是唯一的汉僧代表。

2004年5月，应日本感谢基金会邀请，法师率中国宗教代表团赴瑞士日内瓦参加"关注儿童的宗教者全球网络"第二次世界论坛会议，并做了题为《不同宗教不同教派携起手来　为儿童缔造更加美好的明天》的主题发言。

In July 2004, Master led a delegation to visit Sri Lanka again and was cordially received by President Kumaratunga and Prime Minister Mahinda Rajapaksa. This visit promoted friendship and mutual exchange of Buddhist culture between the two countries.

In February 2005, Master was invited by the Multicultural Association of Indonesia to attend the First International Conference of Multi-religious Education on Peace and Harmony in Jakarta on behalf of China Committee on Religion and Peace. He made a keynote speech entitled "Let the World Be More Harmonious and Beautiful with the Existence of Many Religions". During the visit, Master was cordially received by Suslio Bambang Yudhoyono, President of Indonesia. From November 16th to December 6th, 2005, Master led a Chinese Buddhist delegation to Indonesia again to celebrate the 55th anniversary of the establishment of diplomatic relations between China and Indonesia. They attended the Dharma Assembly for Transmitting Three Platforms of Complete Precepts. It was the first time that the Three Platforms of Complete Precepts were transmitted in 500 years in Indonesia.

▶ 2006 年 8 月 在日本第八届世界宗教者和平会议上发言
Giving a speech at the 8th World Assembly of Religions for Peace. August 2006

2004 年 7 月，法师受命率团再次访问斯里兰卡，得到库马拉通加总统及马辛达·拉贾·巴克萨总理的亲切接见。此次访问活动增进了两国人民之间的友谊，促进了两国佛教文化的交流。

2005 年 2 月，应印度尼西亚多元文化协会的邀请，法师代表中国宗教界和平委员会参加了在雅加达召开的第一届"多宗教和平与和谐教育国际研讨会"，并做了《让世界因多元宗教的存在而更加和谐更加美丽》的主题发言，受到印度尼西亚苏西洛总统的亲切接见。2005 年 11 月 16 日至 12 月 6 日，为庆祝我国与印度尼西亚建交 55 周年，法师率中国佛教代表团赴印度尼西亚参加传授三坛大戒法会，这是印度尼西亚 500 年来第一次传授三坛大戒。

▶ 2006 年 4 月 14 日 在浙江杭州首届世界佛教论坛上发言
Giving a speech at the 1st World Buddhist Forum, Hangzhou, Zhejiang. April 14th, 2006

From April 13th to 16th 2006, Buddhist Association of China and China Religious Culture Communication Association successfully co-sponsored the First World Buddhist Forum in Hangzhou and Zhoushan, Zhejiang Province. Master worked whole-heartedly and conscientiously from the preparation to its successful ending. At this grand gathering, Master delivered a speech entitled "A Harmonious World Begins with Our Minds". He said, "The Buddhist Association of China and the fourfold assembly of Buddhist disciples at large seek to build a harmonious society in China. We hold on to the principle of embodying the universal love in the traditional Chinese culture, 'When one wishes to establish himself, he helps others to establish themselves first; what one wishes to achieve for himself, he helps others to achieve first.' We sincerely appeal to all Buddhists, 'A harmonious world begins with our minds', though we may be from different countries, ethnic groups, or sects. Let's unite with people all over the world and work together to build a harmonious world of long-lasting peace and common prosperity."

On May 6th, 2006, Master was invited by the Government of Thailand and Mahachulalongkornrajavidyalaya University to lead a delegation to Thailand and attend the 3rd United Nations Day of Vesak International Buddhist Conference. From August 26th to 29th of the same year, Master was invited to Japan to attend the 8th World Assembly of Religions for Peace where he gave a speech entitled "Let Us Share Religious Wisdom, Security and Peace" on behalf of the religious community of China. He said, "We pray that the world's religions join hands to make religion a beacon of human spiritual life, leading the boat of human beings to bypass the rocks of raging violence, veer from the erroneous areas of social injustice, polarization of wealth, ecological deterioration and confrontation of civilizations. Let man reach the other side of the shore where the ideal is real; where it is secure, auspicious and peaceful; where people treat others as they would like to be treated themselves. Let the world share religious wisdom, share the peace and security!"

On October 26th of the same year, Master led a Chinese Buddhist delegation with over 120 people to Japan to attend the 9th China, Korea and Japan Buddhist Friendly Exchange Conference held in Kyoto. On behalf of the Chinese delegation, Master made a speech entitled "Same World, Same Action and Aspiration".

From February 5th to 12th, 2007, Master led a Chinese Buddhist delegation of more than 70 people to Bihar, India, to attend the inaugural ceremony for the Xuanzang Memorial Hall upon completion of its renovation. The ceremony included representatives

2006 年 4 月 13 日至 16 日，在浙江杭州及舟山市，中国佛教协会与中华宗教文化交流协会成功协办了首届世界佛教论坛。从筹备到圆满结束，法师始终尽心尽力，认真负责。在此盛会期间，法师代表中国佛教界做了题为《和谐世界　从心开始》的大会主题发言，他说："中国佛教协会以及广大佛教四众弟子，在力求于国内构建和谐社会的同时，秉承着中国传统文化'己欲立而立人，己欲达而达人'的博爱精神，发出'和谐世界，从心开始'的热切呼吁，倡议不同国家、不同民族、不同宗派的佛教徒与世界各国人民一道为构建一个持久和平、共同繁荣的和谐世界而共同努力。"

2006 年 5 月 6 日，应泰国政府和朱拉隆功佛教大学的邀请，法师率团赴泰参加第三届"卫塞节"国际佛教会议。同年 8 月 26 日至 29 日，法师应邀赴日本参加第八届世界宗教者和平会议，并代表中国宗教界做了《共享宗教智慧　共享安全和平》的大会发言。他说："祈愿世界各大宗教携起手来，使宗教成为人类精神生活的灯塔，引领人类之舟绕过暴力肆虐的礁石，驶出社会不公、贫富分化、生态恶化、文明对抗的误区，到达安全祥和、视人如己的理想彼岸。让世界人民共享宗教智慧，共享和平安全！"

同年 10 月 26 日，法师率中国佛教代表团 120 多人，再次赴日本参加于京都举行的第九届中韩日佛教友好交流会议。在大会上法师代表中方做了题为《同一个世界　同一种行愿》的演讲。

2007 年 2 月 5 日至 12 日，法师率中国佛教代表团 70 余人，赴印度参加中印两国政府和佛教界代表在印度比哈尔邦举行的玄奘纪

from both Indian and Chinese governments and Buddhist communities. At the ceremony, Master was the presiding monk of the ceremony who took and offered incense. He said, "We hold this grand gathering to sincerely commemorate Ven. Master Xuanzang. We cherish our memory of this friendship ambassador between Chinese and Indian peoples and strive to deepen our friendship. This ceremony will promote the development and prosperity of Buddhism, strengthening the goodness within human minds and advancing world harmony." On February 27th, 2007, Master welcomed President of Sri Lanka, Mahinda Rajapaksa, at Lingguang Temple, Beijing. On May 22nd, Master was invited by the Thailand-China Buddhist Culture Research Center of Thailand, the Buddhist Association of Thailand and the Day of Vesak Organizing Committee of the United Nations to lead a delegation to Thailand. They attended the Thailand-China Art Exhibition "The World of Buddhist Paintings" and the 2007 United Nations Day of Vesak activities.

▶ 2007 年 2 月 12 日 在印度为玄奘纪念堂重缮落成开光主法
Hosting the inauguration of Xuanzang Memorial Hall upon completion of its renovation, India. February 12th, 2007

念堂修复完缮落成典礼。在典礼上，法师主法拈香，他说："我们在此举行盛会，真诚地纪念玄奘大师，缅怀这位中印两国人民友好的大使，加深我们的友谊，对于促进世界佛教的发展、兴盛，推动人心的和善以及世界的和谐，必将产生积极而深远的影响。"2月27日，法师在北京灵光寺又接待了斯里兰卡总统马辛达·拉贾·巴克萨一行。5月22日，应泰国泰中佛教文化研究中心、泰国佛教协会以及联合国"卫塞节"组委会之邀请，法师率团前往泰国进行访问，出席泰中"佛画世界"艺术联展暨2007年联合国"卫塞节"活动。

▶ 2007 年 5 月 26 日 在泰国第四届联合国卫塞节上发言
Giving a speech at the United Nations Day of Vesak, Thailand. May 26th, 2007

In September 2007, Master was invited to the Great Hall of the People to participate in the Celebration of the 50th Anniversary of the establishment of the Chinese Taoist Association. At the conference, he said, "As everyone knows, China is a country with many faiths. After nurturing, development, absorption and integration through a very long history, a sense of religious coexistence has come into being. 'The movement of heaven is full of power, thus the man of virtue makes himself strong and untiring. The earth is receptive and harmonious, thus the man of profound virtue holds the world.' Let the five major religions of China strive for the prosperity of the motherland and peace among mankind."

On October 26th, 2007, the 10th China, Korea and Japan Buddhist Friendly Exchange Conference was held in Beijing. The theme of the conference was "To Promote World Harmony with the Wisdom of the Buddha". Master made the keynote speech entitled "To Promote World Harmony is the Sacred Duty of Buddhists". He said, "Since ancient times, the fundamental requirements of Buddha's Teachings have remained constant: from purifying people's minds to raising their moral quality; from improving harmony within family, community and society to contributing to constructing a harmonious world. These are also the vivid manifestation of the Buddha's compassion for benefiting the world. When the mind is pure, so is the world. The Buddhists in our three countries should make their own efforts and exploration to promote world harmony, purify the minds of mankind, serve society and improve upon life education and moral integrity."

From April 18th to 21st, 2008, on behalf of the Buddhist community, Master participated in the First Chinese Culture Forum in Macao. The representatives of Confucianism, Buddhism and Taoism held a historic dialogue. Amidst the dialogue, Master said, "Buddhism has been disseminated in China for more than two thousand years. It has integrated itself into traditional Chinese culture and every aspect of Chinese society, as well as the blood of Chinese descendants, becoming one of the three backbones of traditional Chinese culture."

On July 16th, 2008, Master, with a delegation, participated in the World Conference on Dialogue hosted by the World Muslim League in Madrid, Spain. He delivered a speech entitled "Let Us Carry out Multi-religious Dialogues and Jointly Build a Harmonious

2007 年 9 月，法师应邀赴人民大会堂，参加中国道教协会成立 50 周年庆祝大会。在大会上，他说："众所周知，中国是一个拥有多元宗教信仰的国家，各种宗教经过长期的孕育发展、吸纳融通，形成了多元共存、和睦相处的格局。'天行健，君子以自强不息；地势坤，君子以厚德载物。'让我们五大宗教齐心协力，奋发向上，为祖国的繁荣昌盛，为人类的和平事业携手并进，共创未来。"

2007 年 10 月 26 日，第十次中韩日佛教友好交流会议在北京隆重举行。此次会议的主题是"以佛陀的智慧，促进世界和谐"。法师做了《促进世界和谐是佛教徒的神圣职责》的基调发言。他说："自古至今，无论是净化人心、提高民众的道德素质，还是促进家庭、社区、社会的和谐，乃至推动构建和谐世界，本来就是佛教教义的根本要求，也是佛陀慈悲济世精神的生动体现。心清净，故世界清净，促进世界范围内的和谐，净化人心，服务社会，加强生命教育和道德建设，三国佛教徒应为此做出各自的努力与探索。"

2008 年 4 月 18 日至 21 日，法师代表佛教界参加了在澳门举办的首届文明对话暨论坛，儒释道三家的代表人物进行了历史性的对话。在对话当中，法师说："佛教在中国流传超过两千年的时间，已经融入到中华传统文化以及中国社会的方方面面，也融入到炎黄子孙的血液当中，成为中华传统文化的三大主干之一。"

2008 年 7 月 16 日，法师随团赴西班牙的马德里参加伊斯兰世界联盟主办的世界对话大会，并做了《开展多元宗教对话　共同建设和谐世界》的主题发言。法师在发言中说："世界各大宗教都拥

World". In his speech, Master said, "All the major religions of the world have their own great teachings which are of ever new and eternal value to human beings. Religious wisdom should not be limited to being the moral and ethical standards within one religion, country, ethnic group or community. More importantly, it should reflect the moral and ethical standards of different religions, ethnic groups and countries. Dialogue promotes harmony and peace. Dialogue also highlights diversity." Master summarized his views on this conference as "avoiding exclusiveness, respecting other religions, reflecting inclusiveness and promoting harmony." Before and after the opening ceremony, Master accepted television interviews with Middle Eastern countries such as Saudi Arabia, Kuwait and the United Arab Emirates as well as European countries such as the United Kingdom and Spain. During such interviews, Master emphasized the significance of inter-faith dialogue for interpersonal harmony, social harmony and world peace.

► 2007 年 10 月 26 日 在北京第十届中韩日佛教友好交流会议上发言
Giving a speech at the 10th China, Korea and Japan Buddhist Friendly Exchange Conference, Beijing. October 26th, 2007

有那些历久弥新，对人类具有永恒价值的伟大教导。作为世界上各大宗教共同启示的宗教智慧，不应当只是一个国家、一个民族、一个宗教、一个团体内部成员之间的道德伦理准则，更重要的它也是不同宗教、不同民族、不同国家之间的道德伦理准则。对话促进和谐与和睦，对话也更突出多元性。"法师对这次大会的观感概括为："拒绝排他，尊重异教；体现包容，促进和谐。"大会开幕仪式前后，法师接受了沙特、科威特、阿联酋等阿拉伯国家及英国、西班牙等欧洲国家的电视台采访。主要强调了当今世界开展多元宗教对话对建设人际和睦、社会和谐、世界和平的人类社会的重要意义。

▶ 2008 年 7 月 18 日 在西班牙世界对话大会上发言
Giving a speech at the 4th World Conference on Dialogue, Spain. July 18th, 2008

From October 9th to 11th, 2008, the 11th China, Korea and Japan Buddhist Friendly Exchange Conference was held in Jeju with the theme of "The Responsibilities of Buddhists for the Protection of the Environment". Master led a delegation of 130 members to attend the conference and delivered a keynote speech entitled "Let Buddhist Values Be Widely Heard Among World Cultures". He said, "The root of the serious global environmental problems is the greed of mankind. As Buddhists, we should seek to find the source of wisdom in the profound Teachings of Buddhism and take the responsibility of protecting earth's ecology together with people from all walks of life. Advocating Buddhist environmental ethics, thoughts and practices are significant to rectifying the misconceptions of humans, improving their environmental ethics and upholding a greener lifestyle." On October 17th, Master and the Chinese religious delegation attended the 7th Asia Conference on Religions and Peace held in Manila, the capital of the Philippines.

From March 28th to April 1st, 2009, the 2nd World Buddhist Forum was held in Wuxi, Jiangsu Province and Taipei. The Forum was co-organized by Buddhist Association of China and China Religious Culture Communication Association. Master worked very hard during the whole process from preparation to conclusion to bring forth a successful forum. Just a few days before the opening of the Forum, Master worked from early in the morning until late at night and suffered from facial paralysis due to overexertion. According to the doctor, it was caused by fatigue and cold wind. The doctor said the treatment would take one month and the recovery would take three months, but there could also be some after-effects. The doctor suggested that Master should not go outdoors for the next three months. However, for the sake of the Forum and to benefit living beings, Master arrived in Wuxi on March 24th.

During this event, on behalf of the Chinese Buddhist community, Master made a keynote speech entitled "Harmony Needs Conditions, Conditions are Indispensable for Harmony". He said, "Today, the people of the world are a mutually dependent life unity with their destinies entwined. All countries, organizations, religions and individuals should jointly address global problems such as the financial crisis, ecological crisis and climate crisis. Harmony needs conditions; conditions are indispensable for harmony. In

2008 年 10 月 9 日至 11 日，第十一次中韩日三国佛教友好交流会议在韩国济州岛举行。此次会议主题为"佛教徒为环境保护所承担的责任"。法师率 130 人的大型代表团赴会，并在大会上做了《让佛教的价值观放声于世界文化的体系中》的会议基调发言。他说："全球范围内严重的环境问题之所以产生，其根源是人类的贪心。身为一名佛教徒，我们应当从佛教博大精深的教义中寻求智慧的源泉，与各界人士共同担负起保护地球生态的重大责任。提倡佛教环境伦理思想及其实践活动，对于匡正人类的偏差观念，提高人类的环境伦理道德，促成人们崇尚环保的生活方式，具有重大的意义。"10 月 17 日，法师随中国宗教界代表团赴菲律宾首都马尼拉参加第七届亚洲宗教和平会议。

2009 年 3 月 28 日至 4 月 1 日，第二届世界佛教论坛在江苏无锡及台北隆重举行。中国佛教协会与中华宗教文化交流协会成功协办了这届论坛。从筹备到圆满结束，法师为这届论坛的成功举办付出了大量心血。在论坛即将开幕的前几天，法师因终日操劳，而得了面瘫。大夫说，致病的因缘是劳累及冷风，治疗期需要一个月，恢复期要三个月，如果这期间不能根治，就会留下后遗症，因此大夫建议三个月不要出门。法师为了论坛、为了众生，仍于 3 月 24 日赶到无锡。

在此盛会期间，法师代表中国佛教界做了题为《和合需要众缘　众缘才能和合》的大会主题发言，他说："今天，世界人类已经是一个唇齿相依、休戚与共的生命整体！面对全球性的金融危机、生态危机、能源危机、气候危机等问题，应该由所有国家、所有组织、所有宗教、所有个人共同来做。和合需要众缘，众缘才能

Buddha's Teachings, there are many thoughts on diversified harmony, as well as systematic guidelines for achieving contentment, compassion, modesty and other virtues. We should explore the fundamental teachings and traditions related to diversity and harmony in Buddhist wisdom, research and practice them more thoroughly and fully, and use them for building a harmonious world."

On July 2nd, 2009, Master went to Astana, Kazakhstan to participate in the 3rd Congress of Leaders of World and Traditional Religions, and made a keynote speech entitled "Enhance Dialogue, Cooperate Closely, Build a Diversified and Harmonious Spiritual Home for Mankind". In his speech, Master said, "Religion is the core of human civilization. A harmonious world begins with harmony among religions. Harmony among religions is the result of dialogue and cooperation. The culture and successful practice that China has accumulated in its long history can provide today's world with the resources for achieving multi-religious harmony. Let every person and every religious believer in the world learn from the wisdom of all religions. Let they enrich and enhance their own

▶ 2009 年 7 月 3 日 接受哈萨克斯坦国家电视台采访
An interview with Kazakhstan TV. July 3rd, 2009

和合！佛教教义中有着丰富的多元和合的思想观念，并有知足、慈悲、谦虚等美德的系统教导。我们应该继承和发掘佛教智慧中多元和合的基本教义和优良传统，通过各种途径和活动更深入、更充分地研究和践行它们，使之成为构建和谐世界的宝贵思想资源。"

2009 年 7 月 2 日，法师随团赴哈萨克斯坦阿斯塔纳参加第三届世界和传统宗教领袖大会，并做了《加强对话　密切合作　共建多元和谐的人类精神家园》的主题发言。法师在发言中说："宗教是人类文明的核心。和谐世界从和谐宗教开始；和谐宗教从对话和合作之中产生。中华民族在悠久历史中积淀下来的深厚文化及成功实践，可以为当今世界如何超越不同宗教在终极信仰上的差异，并达致多元宗教和谐共处提供了重要思想资源和现实启示。让世界上每

▶ 2009 年 7 月 2 日　在哈萨克斯坦出席第三届世界和传统宗教领袖大会
Attending the 3rd Congress of Leaders of World and Traditional Religions, Kazakhstan.
July 2nd, 2009

spiritual state and moral standards, and relieve and ultimately resolve the global crises that all human beings are facing. The realization of a harmonious and compatible human spiritual world needs the unvarying endeavors of all religions. Open-minded and learning-oriented dialogues will be of decisive significance to the exchange of thoughts and the integration of religions. On the basis of dialogues, all religions should also work together and face the sufferings and problems of mankind. Only through the cooperation of mutual trust can we better shoulder the global responsibility. We believe that through this Congress of Leaders of World and Traditional Religions, all religions will be able to learn sincerely from one another and become more open-minded. Different religious groups will be able to cooperate whole-heartedly with more trust. Through our persistent efforts, all religions will tolerate each other, integrate with each other and thus achieve harmony and compatibility. We believe that the world of tomorrow will be more harmonious and beautiful!"

From October 16th to 18th, 2009, the 12th China, Korea and Japan Buddhist Friendly Exchange Conference was held in Yokohama, Japan, with the theme of "Social Responsibility of Buddhism". Master led a 111-member delegation to attend this conference and made a keynote speech entitled "Build the Culture of the Mind for Mankind". He said, "Humanism, individualism, materialism and consumerism are all rooted in the three poisons of the mind: greed, hatred and ignorance. Only a remedy of the mind can cure the disease of the mind. Buddhism is a religion that places extreme emphasis on our minds. The spiritual path of Buddhism is profound and vast, which focuses on turning a mind of ignorance and afflictions into a mind of enlightenment. We should regard 'Culture of the Mind' as our guideline and promote the Buddhist approach of mind purification, that is, diligently practice precepts, concentration and wisdom to vanquish greed, hatred and ignorance. In this way, we facilitate the formation of a new human civilization holding the 'Culture of the Mind' as its main principle, which takes root in the mind and is practiced in society."

一个人、每一个宗教徒都可以汲取所有宗教的智慧成果，丰富和提升自身的精神境界和道德水平，缓解并最终化解人类所面临的全球性危机。实现和谐共容的人类精神世界，需要各宗教付出恒久的努力。开放性的学习型对话，将对各宗教之间的思想交流和融合具有决定意义。各宗教还应在对话的基础上加以合作，携手共同面对人类的苦难与问题，只有进行相互信任的合作才能更好地共同承担全球责任。我们相信，通过这次世界与传统宗教领袖代表会议，各宗教都将能够以更加开放的心态向其他宗教坦诚学习，以更加信任的心态与其他宗教通力合作。经过我们持之以恒的努力，各宗教将实现相互宽容、相互融会，进而达到和谐共容的状态。我们相信，世界的明天一定可以更加和谐、更加美好!"

2009 年 10 月 16 日至 18 日，第十二次中韩日三国佛教友好交流会在日本横滨举行。此次会议主题为"佛教的社会责任"。法师率 111 人的代表团赴会，并在大会上做了《建设人类的心文化》的会议基调发言。他说:"人类中心主义、个人中心主义、物质主义、消费主义皆根植于人类心中的贪、嗔、痴三毒。心病还需心药医。佛教是极为重视'心'的宗教。佛教之道，甚深而广大，究其根本，在明心见性，转无明的烦恼心成为觉悟的菩提心。我们应以'心文化'为主导，弘扬佛教'勤修戒定慧，熄灭贪嗔痴'的心灵净化方法，促使源自内心、践于社会，以'心文化'为核心的人类新文明的形成。"

On October 19th, 2010, the 13th China, Korea and Japan Buddhist Friendly Exchange Conference was held in Lingshan Brahma Palace in Wuxi, China. The subject of this meeting was "Harmonious Spirit of the Golden Tie—In Remembrance of Rev. Zhao Puchu". Master, as the chief representative of China, gave a speech entitled "New Civilization, Culture of the Mind and Harmony of the Mind—Inherit and Develop the Harmonious Spirit of the Golden Tie". He said, "Among oriental Buddhist societies, China, Korea and Japan are in a core position. Therefore, the in-depth exchange and positive cooperation between Buddhist fields in these three countries will have important and profound significance in achieving the historic mission of building the culture and the Harmony of the Mind in a new era of human civilization. It is just the great contribution and value of the Golden Tie of these three countries to the future of human civilization!"

On November 2nd, 2011, the 14th China, Korea and Japan Friendly Buddhist Exchange Conference was held at Naksansa Temple in Gangwon-do, Korea. The theme of the conference was "The Social Value and Influence of Buddhist Culture". Master was the keynote speaker of the conference. In his speech entitled "The Social Value and Influence of Buddhist Culture", he said, "We believe that the grand march towards the inner heart will start the third great revolution of human society. The first revolution happened in Axial Times, when primitive culture made great leaps in religious understanding and began to possess a social ethos centered around Divinity. The second revolution occurred during Modern Times in the West, where Divine Culture was changed into Material Culture and a system of natural science based around rationality was formed. The aim of the third revolution is to turn Material Culture into a Culture of the Mind and establish a mental order with Wisdom of Non-duality. The Wisdom of Non-duality is to try to eliminate the thinking mode of binary opposition. Buddhism respects other cultures and religions sincerely and tries to convey its message of being open and tolerant in a multi-cultural environment, which impresses the world deeply."

　　2010 年 10 月 19 日，第十三次中韩日佛教友好交流会议在中国无锡灵山梵宫召开。此次会议主题为"'黄金纽带'的和谐精神——怀念赵朴初先生"。法师作为中方首席代表在会上发表了题为《新文明　心文化　心和谐——继承和发扬"黄金纽带"的和谐精神》的主题演讲。他说："在东方佛教社会中，中韩日三国处于最核心的地位。所以，中韩日三国佛教界的深入交流与积极合作，对于在新的历史时期，面对新的人类文明，共同构建心文化、创造心和谐这一历史使命，具有更为重要和深远的意义，这也正是三国'黄金纽带'对于未来人类文明的重大贡献与宝贵价值！"

　　2011 年 11 月 2 日，第十四次中韩日佛教友好交流会议在韩国江原道洛山寺举行。此次会议主题为"佛教文化的社会价值和影响"。法师作为中方代表团首席代表在大会上做了《佛教文化的社会价值与影响》的会议基调发言。他说："我们有理由期待，这场朝向内心的伟大进军势必开启人类社会的第三次伟大变革。第一次变革发生在'轴心时代'，即由原始文化转向'神文化'，形成了以宗教为基础的社会道德体系；第二次变革发生在西方近代，由'神文化'转向'物文化'，形成了以理性为基础的自然科学体系；第三次变革则将由'物文化'转向'心文化'，构建以'不二智慧'为基础的自我心智秩序。'不二智慧'所要克服的就是二元对立的思维模式。佛教尊重不同文化和不同信仰的真诚态度，在当今世界的多元化语境之下更显示出重要的现实意义。佛教文化展现出的广大开放性和深度包容性，令世人刮目相看。"

▶ 2009 年 10 月 17 日 在日本出席第十二届中韩日佛教友好交流会
Attending the 12th China, Korea and Japan Buddhist Friendly Exchange Conference in Japan. October 17th, 2009

Chapter Eight

Engaging in Social Charity,
Serving Living Beings

■ Master Xuecheng points out that monks and nuns of the new century should engage in "protecting the spiritual environment", taking on responsibilities of glorifying the country, benefiting sentient beings, and building a "Pure Land in the Human Realm".

■ Master said, "Buddhist charity is not just material, but rather spiritual. Beneficiaries may receive material assistance, as well as a purifying effect in the mind."

第八章

社会公益　服务众生

■ 学诚法师提出，新世纪的僧尼要进行内在的"心灵环保"，以庄严国土、利乐有情、建设"人间净土"为己任。

■ 法师说："佛教的慈善事业不仅仅是物质上的慈善，更是精神上的慈善。受到帮助的人，一方面得到物质的援助，同时心灵也得到净化。"

Master receives wide appreciation as he has made such achievement at so young an age. But he is not intoxicated by it. He said, "Monks should not be too secular. The past achievement is the enemy, the present achievement is the friend and achievement yet to be obtained is the teacher." Master holds a high position, yet he never forgets to study and practice. He is a devout Buddhist, and never forgets to serve his country. For many years he has given fervent support to the Party and the government for implementing religious policies. Meanwhile, at the Dharma assemblies held in monasteries, he has taken initiative in introducing the Party's religious policies, guiding believers to be patriotic to the nation and faithful to Buddhism, observe laws and regulations and to be socially responsible.

Master points out that monks and nuns of the new century should engage in "protecting the spiritual environment", taking on responsibilities of glorifying the country, benefiting sentient beings, and building a "Pure Land in the Human Realm". As a member of CPPCC, Master actively participates in the deliberation and administration of state affairs and takes initiative in reporting social conditions and public opinions. He drafts proposals, puts forward advice and suggestions, studies current affairs and politics, ponders over the future and destiny of Chinese Buddhism and gives timely reports to the Party and government departments at various levels on the new trends and issues in the field of religious affairs. At the same time, Master enthusiastically responds to the call of the Party and the government by taking initiative to lead and organize Buddhists to donate money and materials to relieve poverty and disaster, aid students and those in need and supportng and participating in various social charity efforts.

In his article entitled "The Buddhist Public Welfare Cause and the Building of Its System", Master wrote, "Putting on an ascetic appearance with greed remaining in the heart should not be emulated. Buddhism should revaluate the value of economy. Gains of pure wealth reflects good conduct and a positive livelihood, therefore the more the better. Buddhists should engage in jobs at farms, factories, companies, banks, and so on as long as they are beneficial to the national interest, people's livelihood and happiness."

In 1998, when floods broke out in the Yangtze River and a raging typhoon wreaked havoc in Fujian Province, Master not only organized a Sutra Chanting Prayer Dharma Assembly at Putian Guanghua Monastery for the disaster-stricken areas, but also took the lead in donating money and called on monks and followers to donate money and materials to support the disaster-stricken areas and pass on their love to the people there.

　　如此年轻就有这样的成就，法师自然受到不少赞誉，但他对此都看得平淡如水。他说："出家人不能太俗气。过去的成绩是敌人，现在的成绩是朋友，未来的成绩是老师。"法师身居高位而不忘修学，笃信佛教而不忘报国。多年来，他全力协助党和政府贯彻落实宗教政策，同时在寺院举办的法会上，积极宣传党的宗教政策，引导信众爱国爱教，遵纪守法，保有一颗社会责任心。

　　法师提出，新世纪的僧尼要进行内在的"心灵环保"，以庄严国土、利乐有情、建设"人间净土"为己任。作为全国政协常委，法师积极参政、议政，主动反映社情民意，撰写提案，建言献策，并认真学习时事政治，思考中国佛教的前途与命运，及时向各级党政部门汇报有关宗教领域的动态与问题。同时还积极响应党和政府的号召，主动带领和组织佛教信众捐款捐物、扶贫救灾、助学济困，支持并参与社会各项公益事业。

　　法师在《佛教的公益事业及其教制建设》一文中说道："若是心里的贪欲不除，外表装出苦行的样子，也不足取法。佛教应该重新估定经济的价值，只要是合于正业、正命的净财，应是多多益善；只要能对国家民生、对幸福快乐的生活有所增益的事业，诸如农场、工厂、公司、银行等，佛教徒都应该去做。"

　　1998 年长江洪水爆发，台风肆虐八闽大地时，他不仅以佛教特有的方式在莆田广化寺为灾区举办"诵经祈福法会"，更以实际行动带头捐资，并发动僧众和信徒捐款捐物支持灾区，向灾区人民献出了一份爱心。

In July 2004, Fufeng County in Shaanxi Province suffered flood damage, at a level unprecedented in the past 60 years. Though far in Beijing, when Master Xuecheng heard about the disaster, he phoned immediately for the details, and asked Ven. Zhichao, the Deputy Manager of Famen Monastery, to donate 100,000 RMB to the disaster-stricken areas.

On January 1st, 2005, BAC organized a Cross-Strait Dharma Assembly with a Thousand Monks from a Hundred Monasteries to donate for the relief of the 2004 Tsunami in the Indian Ocean. The Tsunami took place on December 26th, 2004 and struck eight countries including Indonesia, Sri Lanka, India and Thailand. Master Xuecheng presided over the Dharma Assembly and delivered a touching speech with deep and loving concern. "This disaster shocked the whole world. The death toll has reached more than 100,000 people and there are still hundreds of thousands of victims. Moreover, millions of people are unable to get necessary survival supplies. They have neither access to drinking water nor basic sanitation. Food supply is an even bigger problem. We have seen many houses swept away and so many precious lives swallowed up in an instant. How heavy our hearts are at this very moment!" In the Dharma Assembly, Master took the lead in donating money, contributing 10,000 RMB in his own name and 100,000 RMB on behalf of Famen Monastery.

In the period of Chinese New Year Holiday 2005, under the auspices of Master, Famen Monastery organized large poverty relief charity activities, giving 147 homeless elderly citizens at 13 nursing homes rice, flour, oil, calendars, cash and other materials.

In the golden autumn of October 2006, under Master's guidance, a group of lay Buddhists who were committed to charity initiated the establishment of Beijing Ren Ai Charity Foundation. Without abundant fund and existing models, the Foundation started from nothing. Attracted by Master's compassion and vows, many enthusiastic lay Buddhists and warm-hearted people have devoted themselves to Buddhist charity. After its establishment, the Foundation now has charity programs including the Ren Ai Student Project, the Ren Ai Yi+Yi Clothing Donation Project, the Ren Ai Charity Stand Project, the Ren Ai Disaster Relief Project, the Ren Ai Filial Piety Award, the Voice of Longquan Hotline Project and the Care for the Aged Project etc. All of these programs have already directly or indirectly helped many living beings. They have opened a new chapter for Master's endeavors in promoting Dharma and benefiting living beings.

2004 年 7 月，陕西省扶风县遭遇 60 年不遇的水灾，当时远在北京的学诚法师获悉后，立即打电话详细询问灾情，并委托法门寺副监院智超法师向灾区捐款 10 万元。

2005 年 1 月 1 日，中国佛教协会为在 2004 年 12 月 26 日印度洋海啸中遭受巨大灾难的印度尼西亚、斯里兰卡、印度、泰国等八个国家灾民举行了"海峡两岸　百寺千僧　捐款千万　救苦救难法会"，学诚法师主持法会，并发表了情深意切、感人肺腑的讲话："这场举世震惊的灾难，死亡人数已达十多万人，受灾者达几十万人，数百万人无法得到生存所需的物资，他们既没有饮用水，也缺乏基本卫生条件，食品供应更是大成问题。我们看到一座座美丽的家园被惊涛骇浪席卷而走，一个个宝贵的生命被凶狠死神瞬间吞噬，此时此刻，我们的心情是多么沉重！"在法会上，法师以个人名义带头捐献了 1 万元人民币，并代表法门寺捐献了 10 万元赈灾款。

2005 年春节，在法师主持下，法门寺举行了大型慈善济贫活动，为 13 所敬老院的 147 位孤寡老人送去了米、面、油、挂历和慰问金等。

2006 年金秋 10 月，在法师的指导下，一批致力于慈善事业的居士们发起成立了北京市仁爱慈善基金会。基金会没有雄厚的资金，没有现成的模式，一切白手起家。靠着法师的悲愿感召了众多满腔热情的居士和善心人士投身于佛教慈善事业。基金会成立以来，"仁爱助学""仁爱衣＋衣""仁爱心栈""仁爱救灾""仁爱孝德奖""龙泉之声倾听热线""老年关怀"等慈善项目，直接或间接地帮助了许多众生，使法师的弘法利生事业掀开新的篇章。

In March 2007, the Ren Ai Student Project provided financial aid for orphaned students above Grade One in junior high school. In addition, long-term spiritual care has also been given. "Financial aid is the beginning while spiritual care is the focus; financial aid is limited but spiritual care is infinite." This is the ethos of this project. In March 2008, Ren Ai Foundation, in cooperation with the team of EMBA Blue Ribbon Project of Shanghai Transportation University, donated 450,000 RMB to subsidize nearly 200 students in Anhui Province. Apart from Anhui Province, the Ren Ai Student Project has also worked well in Beijing and Hebei Province.

In July 2007, from the very beginning, the Ren Ai Yi+Yi Clothing Donation Project established the sorting and allocation principle to be "one to one, extending care down to the individual", given high expectations for ordinary project of clothing donation. The Foundation allocated and packed clothing for four seasons in accordance with gender, age, height and other traits of the receivers. In October 2008, after five months of elaborate preparation, the Foundation organized a large campaign "Ren Ai Clothing Donation Warms a Myriad of Families" at Dabei Town, Shunping County in Hebei Province, a national level poverty-stricken county and 120,000 articles of clothes were delivered to nearly 6,000 households, benefiting over 20,000 people in 44 villages. In 2008 alone, the Ren Ai Yi+Yi Clothing Donation Project donated more than 420,000 pieces of clothing to earthquake-stricken areas in Sichuan and depressed areas in Hebei, Anhui, Qinghai and Gansu. More than 100,000 people benefited from the project. It is also noteworthy that in 2008 the number of people who participated in the clothing donation and sorting exceeded 50,000 and they were from all different circles of society and different age groups.

In January 2008, the first Ren Ai Charity Stand was set up at the Honglian Zhongli Community in Xuanwu District, Beijing. Every morning, as part of their community service, the Charity Stand serves "love porridge" for free to the "busy people in the city" who have no time for breakfast and lonely elderly citizens, showing care through providing warm porridge.

Volunteers have been serving warm porridge in the bustling streets, sharing their best wishes to those they meet. Rain or shine, workdays or holidays, "love porridge" has been served uninterruptedly for 365 days a year. Serving porridge has been widely publicized by

2007 年 3 月，"仁爱助学"项目面向经济困难的初一以上孤儿学生提供经济资助，更给予长期的心灵呵护。"资助为起点，关怀为重点；资助有限，关爱无限"，正是这一项目的宗旨。2008 年 3 月，仁爱基金会携手上海交通大学 EMBA 蓝丝带项目组捐赠 45 万元，资助近 200 名安徽学生。除安徽省外，"仁爱助学"项目在北京、河北等地都已顺利开展。

2007 年 7 月，本着对捐衣这个普通慈善项目寄予的厚望，"仁爱衣 + 衣"项目从一开始便确立了"一一对应，关怀到人"的衣物分拣和发放原则。基金会根据每一位受助人的性别、年龄和身高等信息逐一配备四季衣物，逐一打包。2008 年 10 月，历经五个月的精心筹备，基金会在国家级贫困县河北省顺平县大悲乡组织了"衣衣仁爱，温暖万家"大型衣物捐赠活动，发放衣物 12 万件，来自 44 个山村，近 6,000 家贫困户的 2 万多名乡亲受益。仅在 2008 年，"仁爱衣 + 衣"项目就捐赠衣物 42 万余件，惠及四川地震灾区，河北、安徽、青海、甘肃等贫困地区，受益者 10 余万人。同样难能可贵的是，2008 年全国各地参与衣物捐赠和分拣的爱心人士超过 5 万人，涵盖社会各个阶层、各个年龄段。

2008 年 1 月，第一家"仁爱心栈"在北京市宣武区红莲中里小区设立。作为便民服务之一，心栈每日清晨免费奉送"爱心粥"，给无暇做早饭的"都市忙人"，以及缺少照顾的孤寡老人们提供方便，并透由一碗热粥，传递关爱。

义工们每日清晨在繁华的大街上给过往的行人奉上热粥，并真诚地道一句美好的祝福。风雨无阻，节假无休，"爱心粥"演绎着

► 2009 年 10 月 6 日 仁爱在安徽太湖举办助学活动
Ren Ai Charity Foundation carrying out Student Project in Taihu, Anhui.
October 6th, 2009

► 2011 年 1 月 8 日 仁爱心栈在北京火车站奉粥
Ren Ai Charity Stand serving porridge at Beijing Railway Station.
January 8th, 2011

► 2011 年 10 月 5 日 法师在北京龙泉寺与老菩萨们共度重阳
Master spending the Double-Ninth Festival for the Elderly with the seniors at
Beijing Longquan Monastery. October 5th, 2011

► 2011 年 10 月 14 日 仁爱在安徽太湖举行孝德奖颁奖活动
Ren Ai Charity Foundation presenting Filial Piety Award in Taihu, Anhui.
October 14th, 2011

the media in Beijing and enthusiastically appreciated by the people of the city. A host of Beijing Television commented, "In the past, porridge was given to relieve famine, but now it is served to deliver warmth."

Although serving porridge is a traditional charity act, the philanthropic connotation it contains has been enduring and is now glowing with vigorous vitality. The Charity Stand has truly become a base for local residents and students to practice caring for others and doing good. Two more Ren Ai Charity Stands have been established later in Tsinghua Science Park and Chaowai SOHO. By January 26th, 2012, a total of 1.26 million cups of porridge have been served, about 1.2 million volunteers have taken part in the project if counted by participation times, and more than 2.76 million people have been benefited. At the 2009 Capital Charity Public Welfare Evening Party, the Ren Ai Charity Stand Project was awarded as an Excellent Charity Project.

In 2008, the Ren Ai Disaster Relief Project started as situation required. In late March, the Dabie Mountain and Tianmu Mountain in southern Anhui Province suffered a serious frost and snow disaster. The volunteers of the Foundation went up and down the hill, visiting to pay condolence to nearly 7,000 households in six districts of Jixi County and Taihu County. They handed out 190,000 kg of rice, more than 50,000 articles of clothes to the household and donated 450,000 RMB to fund education.

On May 12th, Wenchuan suffered heavy loss from a catastrophic magnitude 8 earthquake, which claimed countless lives and left a large number of survivors homeless. Under Master's guidance, Ren Ai Foundation donated more than 5 million RMB worth of relief supplies to disaster-stricken areas at the earliest time possible and opened three temporary schools. On the afternoon of May 28th, Master flew to the earthquake-stricken area in Sichuan Province and with Ven. Master Yicheng, co-chaired the Grand Dharma Assembly of the Chinese Buddhist Community for Praying and Disaster Relief. It was held on the morning of May 29th at Baoguang Monastery in Chengdu, Sichuan Province. They prayed for bliss, deliverance of the dead and relief for the earthquake stricken area. On May 30th and 31st, Master visited and condoled the severely damaged Luohan Monastery, Puzhao Monastery, Erwang Temple, and Ziping Health Clinic in Dujiangyan, as well as schools and other places. Confronted with such a national disaster, Chinese Buddhist society, including those of lay believers, donated more than 300 million RMB.

365 天从不间断的真实故事，奉粥活动也成为京城媒体广为宣传和社会热情称道的善行。一位北京电视台的主持人点评说："过去施粥，赈济的是饥荒；现在奉粥，传递的是温暖。"

奉粥，虽是一个传统的慈善行为，但其真正的慈善内涵依然经久不衰，并焕发出勃勃的生机，真正成为为居民、学生提供身心关怀和实践善行的基地。之后基金会又在清华科技园、朝外 SOHO 相继建立了两家"仁爱心栈"。截止到 2012 年 1 月 26 日，累计奉粥 126 万杯，参与志愿者约 120 万人次，受益者 276 万人。"仁爱心栈"项目在 2009 年的首都慈善公益晚会上获优秀慈善项目奖。

2008 年，"仁爱救灾"项目应运而生。3 月下旬，皖南大别山和天目山区遭受严重雪冻灾害，基金会的义工们翻山越岭，在绩溪和太湖两县境内六地慰问近 7,000 名五保户和低保户，发放大米 38 万斤、衣物 5 万余件，捐赠助学善款 45 万元。

5 月 12 日，汶川发生里氏 8.0 级特大地震，无数生命遇难，大批幸存者无家可归，损失惨重。仁爱基金会在法师的指导下，以最快的速度向灾区捐赠了 500 多万元的救灾物资，开办了 3 所临时学堂。28 日下午，法师飞赴四川地震灾区，同一诚长老等共同主持了 29 日上午在成都宝光寺举行的"中国佛教界为汶川特大地震灾区祈福追荐赈灾大法会"。30 日、31 日，法师走访并慰问了当地受灾严重的罗汉寺、普照寺、二王庙、都江堰紫坪卫生院以及学校等地。面对国家灾难，中国佛教界人士和广大信教群众捐献善款共计 3 亿多元。

On July 7th, xinhuanet.com reported "A donation ceremony for the construction of the biggest teaching facilities in Mianzhu City". For this donation, the Foundation contributed more than 3 million RMB to build schoolhouses for 8 nine-year schools and 7 kindergartens. The net area of the school houses exceeded 8,500 square meters, helping more than 10,000 students and teachers come back into classrooms. The Foundation was honored by the local governments of Sichuan Province as an Advanced Group of Earthquake Relief. It was the only non-governmental charity organization that was awarded such an honor.

Beichuan County was again hit heavily by the earthquake and suffered from debris flow on September 24th, 2008. In the middle of November, the Foundation organized a disaster relief delivery named "Love in Beichuan" in Leigu Town and provided 68 tons of rice, over 40,000 articles of winter clothes and quilts, more than 7,000 pairs of rubber shoes, and more than 1 million RMB worth of medicines for the 2,317 households of the single elderly, the homeless, the disabled, orphaned children and the poor in the 21 villages of Leigu Town. The donation value totaled 2 million RMB and benefited more than 7,800 people.

On April 14th, 2010, a magnitude 7.1 earthquake hit Yushu County in Yushu Tibetan Autonomous Prefecture, Qinghai Province and caused severe casualties and property losses. On that very day, Master instructed the Foundation to prepare some necessities for the disaster-stricken area immediately. At the same time, a Tibetan lay Buddhist Qiusong, a local Ren Ai volunteer had already engaged himself in emergency rescue and disaster relief by going to rescue people at the prayer tower located in the center of Yushu Park. One and a half months later, on June 2nd, Master went to Yushu in person to attend the handover ceremony for the completion and founding of the 3,500 square-meter prefabricated schoolhouses, contributed by the Foundation for the Third Primary School of Yushu.

Since its operation, the Ren Ai Disaster Relief Project has helped people in Anhui, Sichuan, Hebei, Shaanxi, Qinghai, Tibet, Gansu and other places.

On May 24th, 2009, the Ren Ai Filial Piety Award Project was launched. It started in Taihu County, Anhui Province, with the participation of 4,806 students from 7 middle schools. After five months of appraisal and selection, 161 students were issued the Ren Ai

7月7日，新华网报道了"绵竹市最大教学设施举行捐建交接仪式"。此次捐建基金会投资300余万元，为绵竹市八所九年制学校和七所幼儿园捐建板房校舍，使用面积8,500余平方米，帮助1万多名师生重返课堂。基金会被四川当地政府评为"抗震救灾先进集体"，是唯一受此殊荣的纯民间慈善组织。

2008年9月24日，地震重灾区北川县再次遭受泥石流灾害，基金会于11月中旬在擂鼓镇举行了"爱在北川"赈灾物资发放，向擂鼓镇的21个村，2,317户的孤老、孤残、孤童和贫困家庭提供大米68吨、过冬御寒衣被4万余件、胶鞋7,000余双以及价值100多万元的药品，总价值超过200万元，受益群众达7,800余人。

2010年4月14日，青海省玉树藏族自治州玉树县发生7.1级强烈地震，造成重大人员伤亡和财产损失。当天，法师要求基金会立即准备部分灾区必需品。同时，仁爱慈善基金会"仁爱衣＋衣"项目组在玉树当地的藏族志愿者求松居士，已经投入到抢险救援中，在玉树公园中心转经塔一带救人。一个半月之后的6月2日，基金会为玉树第三完全小学捐建的3,500平方米板房校舍全部竣工并交付使用，法师亲自赴玉树参加了交接仪式。

"仁爱救灾"项目自开展以来，救助地区包括安徽、四川、河北、陕西、青海、西藏、甘肃等地。

2009年5月24日，"仁爱孝德奖"项目启动。项目首先在安徽太湖开展，七所中学共4,806名学生参与，经过五个月的评选，基金会正式为161名学生颁发了"仁爱孝德奖"，为21名学生颁发了

Filial Piety Award and 21 students were issued the Ren Ai Filial Piety Star Award by the Foundation. At the end of 2009, this project was awarded as an Excellent Charity Project at the Capital Charity Public Welfare Evening Party.

On July 20th, 2009, under Master's guidance, the Voice of Longquan Hotline was officially launched by the Foundation. Through listening and encouragement, callers were guided to relieve their pressure and recover their self-confidence and happiness. By January 26th, 2012, the Hotline has received 1,935 calls, totaling 1,290 hours, and 206 volunteers have participated in the project successively.

Under Master Xuecheng's guidance, the number of Ren Ai Charity Foundation volunteers, having dedicated their time and enthusiasm selflessly to charity has risen from 4 to over 10,000. The Foundation's charitable projects have benefited several hundred thousand people each year in Beijing alone.

Today the Foundation has been widely recognized by the public. CCTV (China Central Television), BTV (Beijing Television), xinhuanet.com, CNR (China National Radio), *Reference News*, and other mass media networks have given a lot of publicity to the Foundation's charity work. In order to care, understand and help solve the spiritual problems of the public, Master said, "Buddhist charity is not just material, but rather spiritual. Beneficiaries may receive material assistance, as well as a purifying effect in the mind."

During mid-January of 2008, most parts of Southern China and Northwestern China experienced continuous, extreme weather conditions such as large-scale low temperatures, heavy rain, snow and frost. These conditions have been rare since the founding of the PRC. The biggest snowstorm in the past 50 years swept through 14 provinces and municipalities in China, bringing about slippery roads, traffic jams, freezing and splitting of water pipes, power failures, transportation breakdowns and shortage of supplies. Master speedily reported on this and coordinated a Dharma Assembly of Praying for Snow Disaster Alleviation and National Peace at Guangji Monastery, the seat of the Buddhist Association of China. There he also organized a disaster relief donation from Buddhist communities. At the Dharma Assembly, Master said, "The snow disaster has touched all ethnic people's hearts of our country and the hearts of the fourfold assembly of Buddhist disciples. When the Buddhist Association of

"仁爱孝德之星"奖。该项目 2009 年底在首都慈善公益晚会上获优秀慈善项目奖。

2009 年 7 月 20 日，在法师的指导下，基金会的"龙泉之声倾听热线"正式开通。热线志愿者通过倾听、鼓励，引导倾诉者实现心理减压，找回自信和快乐。截止到 2012 年 1 月 26 日，热线话务量 1,935 个，时长 1,290 个小时，相继有 206 位志愿者参与。

在学诚法师的指引下，仁爱慈善基金会从成立之初的 4 名志愿者发展到 1 万多名，他们在慈善领域无私地奉献着自己的时间和热情。仅在北京，基金会的慈善项目每年就要惠及几十万人。

如今基金会已得到了社会的广泛认可。中央电视台、北京电视台、新华网、中央人民广播电台、《参考消息》等众多媒体对基金会的慈善工作均给予了诸多报道。为了关注、了解、帮助解决社会大众心灵方面的诸多问题，法师说："佛教的慈善事业不仅仅是物质上的慈善，更是精神上的慈善。受到帮助的人，一方面得到物质的援助，同时心灵也得到净化。"

2008 年 1 月中旬，我国南方大部分地区和西北地区出现了建国以来罕见的持续大范围低温、雨雪和冰冻的极端天气，一场 50 年不遇的暴风雪席卷我国 14 个省市，致使道路冰滑、交通堵塞、水管冻爆、停电停运、物资紧缺。法师迅速汇报、沟通、协调，在中国佛教协会所在地的广济寺举办"雪灾消弭国泰民安祈福法会"，并组织佛教界捐赠救灾款。在法会上，法师说："雪灾牵动着全国各族人民的心，也牵动着佛教四众弟子的

▶ 2010 年 6 月 1 日 法师在玉树灾区
Master at the disaster-stricken area of Yushu. June 1st, 2010

China learned about the disaster, it immediately notified local Buddhist associations, requested them to take action quickly and contribute themselves to disaster relief in a variety of ways."

On February 8th, Master went to Guizhou to donate 1.71 million RMB to the disaster area on behalf of the Buddhist community. He also donated 10,000 RMB in his own name. At the donation ceremony Master said, "The amount of our donations is insignificant, but the fourfold assembly of Buddhist disciples are doing what we can to help people who live in the disaster-stricken areas. We are deeply concerned with and are paying close attention to the situation, which, in Buddhist terms, is arousing aspiration. In conclusion, we pray with our most pious and pure hearts that the compassionate light of the Three Jewels—the Buddha, Dharma and Sangha—embraces all people of Guizhou Province."

In the early morning of August 22nd, 2009, a magnitude 5.6 earthquake occurred in the offshore areas of South Taiwan. It was the second strongest earthquake since Typhoon Morak inflicted massive devastation upon South Taiwan. Innumerable lives died and there were heavy losses suffered. Master actively engaged himself in organizing donations amongst Buddhist communities. Over 10 million RMB was contributed by the Buddhist community in Mainland China and many Dharma assemblies were organized across the country to pray for the disaster-stricken people in Taiwan and help them get through the disaster. He said, "The donation made by the mainland Buddhist community is a

▶ 2008 年 2 月 1 日　在南方雪灾祈福法会上发言
Giving a speech at the Dharma Assembly for South China Snow Disaster Alleviation and
Eradication. February 1st, 2008

心。中国佛教协会得悉灾情后，立即发出通知，要求各地佛教协会
积极行动起来，以各种方式为抗灾救灾工作做出贡献。"

2 月 8 日，法师代表佛教界到贵州，向灾区捐款 171 万元。法
师还以个人名义捐款 1 万元。在捐赠仪式上法师说："虽然款项微
不足道，但也算是中国佛教四众弟子，为灾区人民尽绵薄之力。我
们是从内心深处，关注、重视这件事的，用佛教的语言来讲，即是
发心。最后我们以最虔诚、最清净的心，祈愿'佛、法、僧'三宝
慈光，加被贵州全省人民。"

2009 年 8 月 22 日清晨，台湾南部近海发生里氏 5.6 级地震，
这已是"莫拉克"台风重创南台湾之后，台湾地区发生的第二次
较强地震。无数生灵遇难，损失很大。法师积极投入组织佛教界
的捐赠工作。大陆佛教界共捐赠 1,000 多万元人民币，并在全国
各地举办多场法会，为台湾受灾民众消灾祈福。他说："大陆佛教

profound expression of the flesh and blood relationship between the mainland Buddhist communities and the people of Taiwan. We share the same roots, the same ancestry, the same vein and the same origins."

One evening in 2008, Master told his attendant, "I am thinking of how the nearly 100 kinds of Buddhist books that we print can benefit the whole public and not only those lay Buddhists who come to the Monastery to study. We can set up a foundation to share these books with the public through means such as major websites..."

Two years later, under Master's guidance, Beijing Great Sinology Foundation was set up on January 26th, 2010, with the approval of the government. The aim of the Foundation is to promote Chinese culture and build a common spiritual homeland for the Chinese nation. The major task of the Foundation is to offer free publications of traditional Chinese cultural classics distributed by leading domestic publishers, especially books on Buddhism, and to carry out domestic and international cultural exchanges.

At present, Beijing Great Sinology Foundation cooperates with Amazon.cn, the world's largest Chinese shopping website, and dangdang.com to provide readers with discounted and free books. Many pages on amazon.cn show discount-related information and link to resources about Beijing Great Sinology Foundation. The books discounted by the Foundation, such as *The Diamond Sutra*, rank around No. 30 on the sales list of the million books sold at amazon.cn. They are the best sellers on traditional Chinese culture and religions available there. According to the statistics of amazon.cn, every day more than 10,000 people visit related columns and only in two months, more than 1 million people have browsed relevant columns. This has been a new and modern shortcut to the large-scale promotion of Buddhism and traditional Chinese culture.

The rejuvenation of the Chinese nation requires a great rejuvenation of Chinese culture. Under Master's guidance, Beijing Great Sinology Foundation will play an important role in exploring Chinese cultural resources, developing a brand name of Chinese culture, building a bridge for Chinese culture and promoting the international influence of Chinese culture.

界的捐赠，是大陆佛教界与台湾同胞同根同祖、同脉同源的骨肉深情的深刻表达。"

2008 年的一个晚上，法师跟随身侍者谈道："我在想，咱们印刷的近百种佛教书籍，如何让社会大众受益，而不是仅仅来寺庙的居士才能学习。我们可以成立一个基金会，通过各大网站等正规渠道公开向社会赠送这些书籍……"

时代的召唤，历史的使命，两年之后的 2010 年 1 月 26 日，在法师的关心指导下，北京复兴大国学文化基金会经国家相关部门正式批准成立，其宗旨为弘扬中华文化，建设中华民族共有精神家园；主要业务为向公众大规模无偿赠送国内权威出版社出版发行的以佛教经典书籍为主的中华传统文化经典，并开展海内外文化交流活动等。

目前，大国学基金会正和全球最大的中文购物网站卓越亚马逊、当当网合作，进行助买、赠送等活动，卓越亚马逊的多个页面显示大国学基金会的助买信息和专题链接，让更多的人从中受益。基金会助买的图书《金刚经》等在卓越百万种图书销量榜三十位上下浮动。在国学类、宗教类都位居第一。据卓越统计，每日有 1 万多人来相关专题访问，仅两个月就有 100 多万人浏览相关专题，这次活动为佛学、国学的大规模弘扬开辟了又一个新的现代化的捷径。

中华民族的伟大复兴，需要中华文化的伟大复兴。法师指导下的北京复兴大国学文化基金会对发掘中华文化资源，打造中华文化品牌，搭建中华文化桥梁，提升中华文化的国际影响，定会发挥重要的作用。

Chapter Nine

The Dawn of the New Century,
Illuminating the Minds of All

■ In view of current situations, Master Xuecheng, with his wisdom and insight, advocates that Buddhist sects should be moderated and that operation should be enhanced to create a harmonious Sangha.

■ In the view of Master, if religion should play a significant role, exert its influence and make contributions in a harmonious society, it must keep up with the times and trace the theme of development; it must approach the realities of contemporary China; it must find concern for the various problems arising from social development; it must respond to the major issues that emerge from social progress.

第九章

世纪曙光　普照十方

■　学诚法师以他睿智的眼光，审时度势，提倡佛教内部应淡化宗派观念，强化组织运作，创建和合僧团。

■　法师认为，宗教要在和谐社会中发挥作用、产生影响、做出贡献，就必须紧跟时代发展的脉搏，贴近当代中国的实际，关切社会发展所产生的种种问题，回应时代进步所提出的重大课题。

Master Xuecheng has always attended to the future and destiny of Chinese Buddhism, Chinese religion and Chinese culture. In Master's view, the birth of religion is an important indication that human society has advanced from ignorance to civilization. He believes that religion is the nucleus and soul of human civilization and a spiritual resource for constructing a harmonious society. If religion should play a significant role, exert its influence and make contributions in a harmonious society, it must keep up with the times and trace the theme of development; it must approach the realities of contemporary China; it must find concern for the various problems arising from social development; it must respond to the major issues that emerge from social progress. In the 21st century where economy is highly developed and people's material lives have greatly improved, cultural and ethical progress will certainly become more and more valued. People have a growing need for religion and Buddhism to solve various problems in their spiritual world and achieve mental balance. If a culture or a value system wants to be recognized, understood and appreciated by other nations, civilizations or people of other countries, it must possess universal values, which transcend political systems or ideologies. It must have a global vision, which stretches beyond a nation, a civilization, a country and one's own interests. It should be said that Chinese Buddhism with its three language families as well as Chinese culture as a whole have both such values and vision. It is only with such values and vision that they can be favored in the 21st century and play a greater role in society, in the reconstruction of Chinese culture and even in the reconstruction of the cultures of all humanity.

Master has given elaborate consideration to the following issues: What kind of role will Chinese Buddhism play in the 21st century; how it can be compatible with a socialist society; how can religion make positive contributions to facilitating social harmony; how to fully implement the fundamental religious policies of the Party and enable religious figures and believers to play a positive role in promoting economic development and social harmony; how to enable religious figures and believers to play a positive role in promoting cultural development; how to inherit and enhance the excellent traditions of Buddhism and absorb the new knowledge of modern times, while building a quality Buddhist Sangha; how to uphold the Dharma, dignify our country, and create bliss, benefits and harmony

　　学诚法师始终关注着中国佛教乃至中国宗教、中国文化的前途和命运。法师认为，宗教的产生是人类社会从蒙昧走向文明的重要标志；宗教是人类文明的核心和灵魂；宗教是构建和谐社会的独特精神资源，宗教要在和谐社会中发挥作用、产生影响、做出贡献，就必须紧跟时代发展的脉搏，贴近当代中国的实际，关切社会发展所产生的种种问题，回应时代进步所提出的重大课题。在经济文化高度发达的 21 世纪，人民的物质生活水平普遍提高，精神文明的建设必将越来越受到重视。人们对宗教、对佛法有着越来越多的需求，以此解决精神世界的种种问题，达到心灵层面的自我平衡。一种文化、一种价值观要得到其他民族、其他文明、其他国家人民的认同、理解与欣赏，必须具有超越政治制度、意识形态的普世价值，必须具有超越一个民族、一个文明、一个国家、一己私利的世界视野。应该说，囊括三大语系的中国佛教乃至整个中国文化具有这样的价值和视野，也只有具备这样的价值和视野，才会赢得 21 世纪人类的青睐，在社会生活中发挥更大的作用，在中国文化乃至全人类文化的重建中扮演更为重要的角色。

　　中国佛教在 21 世纪将会扮演怎样的角色；佛教如何与社会主义社会相适应；如何发挥宗教在促进社会和谐方面的积极作用；如何全面贯彻党的宗教工作基本方针，发挥宗教界人士和信教群众在促进经济发展、社会和谐中的积极作用；如何发挥宗教界人士和信教群众在促进文化繁荣发展中的积极作用；如何继承和发扬佛教优良传统并吸纳现代各种有益的新知识，塑造佛教僧伽良好品格与形象；如何住持正法、庄严国土，真正为众生创造利乐与和谐；如何使佛教善为大众所接受；佛教各宗派之间，佛教与其他宗教之间，

for sentient beings; how to make virtues encouraged by Buddhism naturally accepted by the public; how to carry out communications and dialogues among various sects of Buddhism, between Buddhism and other religions, between the religious society and the significant fields beyond religion such as politics, economics, culture, education, etc.

It is stated in his article "A Brief Talk on the Cultural Construction of Chinese Buddhism" that "Buddhism is a religion with faith as its root, liberation from cyclic existence as its goal, education as its core and culture as its linking tie." In view of current situations, Master, with his wisdom and insight, advocates that Buddhist sects should be moderated and that operation should be enhanced to create a harmonious Sangha. He said, "Buddhist societies, especially the Sangha which is the major body to promote Dharma and uphold Buddhism, always play a decisive role in shaping the destiny of Buddhism." In addition, he stated, "The Sangha should uphold Dharma and the laity should protect and support Dharma. This is the responsibility and obligation of all Buddhists. With the orderly cooperation system of the Sangha and laity, we need to adjust our ideas, keep up with the times and rely on monasteries to face and develop favorable relationships with living beings. We also need to promote Dharma with multiple means that meet the needs of society. We need to manifest the compassion and wisdom of Buddhism, allow society to accept Buddhism, solve practical problems and deliver sentient beings through skillful means. Only when such practical matters have been truly attended for the sake of Buddhism and sentient beings, can new hopes be brought to society of this era."

Concerning society, Master wrote in his article "Religious Concerns about Globalization" that "The expansion and deepening of the world market and the formation and development of transportation and information networks have accelerated the process of globalization, especially economic globalization. This is an inevitable result of the development of modern productivity. Globalization is not an option but a reality and an objective trend. 'The Golden Rules' shared by major religions as their common features: mercy, love, kindness, compassion, forgiveness and mutual assistance, are the source and foundation of global ethics." Master said, "How can we efficiently transform the sources of Chinese Buddhist culture to a realistic soft power? How can we bring into play Chinese Buddhist culture's unique influence, persuasiveness and attractiveness? Buddhists often say,

乃至与整个宗教界与国家政治、经济、文化、教育等各个领域应怎样进行沟通与对话等，法师都做了仔细的思考。

他在《略论中国佛教的文化建设》一文中写道："佛教是一种以信仰为根本、解脱为目的、教育为中心、文化为纽带的宗教。"法师以他睿智的眼光，审时度势，提倡佛教内部应淡化宗派观念，强化组织运作，创建和合僧团。他说："教团，尤其是出家僧众，作为弘扬佛法、住持佛教的主体，始终是决定佛教命运的关键。"另外，法师说："出家众住持佛法，在家众护持佛法，这是大家的责任和义务。有了僧俗有序的配合体系，我们就要调整观念，与时俱进，以道场为依托，面对众生，广结善缘，用符合时空因缘，适应社会需要的、多元化的方式去弘扬佛法，体现佛教悲智的精神，让社会认可佛教，切实解决具体问题，善巧方便度化众生。做出这些实际的事情，真真实实为佛教、为众生考虑，才能给这个时代的人类社会带来新的希望。"

对社会，他在《宗教关注全球化问题》一文中写道："世界市场的扩大和深化，交通、信息网络化的形成和发展，加速了全球化特别是经济全球化的进程，它是现代生产力发展的必然结果。全球化不是一种选择而是一种现实，一种客观趋势。而各大宗教所共同具备并构成共同特征的'黄金法则'（慈悲、仁爱、善意、同情、宽恕、互助）是全球伦理的价值基础和价值源头。"法师说："那如何使中国佛教文化的资源有效地转换成现实的文化软实力，如何让中国佛教文化发挥它特有的感召力、说服力、吸引力？佛教徒常有一句话说：'弘法为家务，利生为事业'。弘法，讲究权巧智能、方

'Promoting Dharma is our household task and benefiting sentient beings is our mission.' Promoting Dharma requires skills and intelligence as well as expedient methods, while for benefiting sentient beings we must consider the needs of people. Both promoting Dharma and benefiting sentient beings will only be achieved through excellent organization and thorough planning."

Master Xuecheng often says, "The future of Buddhism lies in everyone's effort. Start with oneself, start from now on and start from this moment, as benefiting others is the real meaning of life." This young "elder" has been working hard day and night, sparing no effort in establishing a learning and practice system for Han Buddhism. He strives to establish the Buddhist system of faith, ethos, human resources, organization and education as well as to build up a pure, harmonious and progressive team consisting of teachers, teachings and companions. "I offer my deep resolve to serve all beings in the world; this is the way to return Buddha's benevolence." As stated in *Engaging in the Bodhisattva Deeds*, "For as long as space endures and for as long as the world lasts, may I live to dispel the miseries of the world." Master is making unremitting endeavors with his profound and vast compassionate vows and wisdom, leading the Sangha and lay Buddhists to carry forward the great cause of spreading the Dharma and benefiting all sentient beings.

便法门；利生，要考虑社会大众的需要。不论弘法或利生，都必须透过良好的组织与完整的规划，才能顺利地达成。"

学诚法师常说："佛教的未来靠大家一起来承担，从我做起、从现在做起、从当下做起，因为利他才是生命的真正意义。"这位年轻的"长者"为了建立汉传佛教的修学体系，为了佛教的信仰建设、道风建设、人才建设、组织建设、教制建设，为了创建师法友清净和合增上的团队，终日耕耘不辍、呕心沥血。"将此深心奉尘刹，是则名为报佛恩。"正如《入菩萨行论》中所说："乃至有虚空，以及众生住，愿吾住世间，尽除众生苦。"学诚法师正以他深广的悲愿和智慧，带领着僧俗二众，在弘扬佛法、利益众生的伟大事业中不懈努力着。

Afterword

February 29th (the eighth day of the second month of the lunar calendar), 2012 will be my most respected teacher, Ven. Master Xuecheng's 30th anniversary of entering monkhood. To commemorate this special and extraordinary event, I aspired to revise *Stories of Ven. Master Xuecheng* and publish it as a tribute to Venerable Master's profound kindness for teaching me the Dharma. May my teacher enjoy good health and long life to turn the Wheel of Dharma.

It was in the beginning of 2002 that I met with the Venerable Master for the first time at Guanghua Monastery at Nanshan of Putian, Fujian. I was asked to be the accountant monk of Guanghua Monastery by the Venerable Master in early 2003. This gave me more opportunities to be with him. On the Chinese New Year Day in 2004, I was fortunate to move with the Venerable Master to Famen Monastery in Shaanxi Province. It was a very pleasant surprise that I was chosen to be the Venerable Master's attendant on this day, thus allowing me to spend more time with him. I was profoundly influenced by the Venerable Master's virtues in those moments. While I continued to learn about his merits, I came to admire my teacher more and more as time went by.

When the website of Famen Monastery was updated in July of 2004, Wang Yuping, who was in charge of the website, asked me if I could provide a brief introduction to the Venerable Master. Considering its importance, I checked many websites, newspapers and periodicals and found only a few outdated reports about him. Putting the only existing information on the new website seemed insufficient for a virtuous person like him. It so happened that at that time, I was reading and greatly inspired by the biographies of eminent masters, and decided to draft an introduction myself. I started on July 3rd and finished it on July 6th, 2004, with a total of 8,570 characters.

后记

2012 年 2 月 29 日（农历二月初八），是恩师^上学^下诚大和尚出家 30 周年纪念日。在这殊胜的时空因缘下，慧空发愿重新修订《学诚大和尚侧记》予以出版，以兹纪念，并报答师长对弟子的法乳深恩于一毫。祈愿师长：法体安康，长久住世，法轮常转！

慧空于 2002 年初首次在福建莆田南山广化寺值遇和尚，2003 年初被和尚安排为广化寺常住会计，亲近和尚的次数开始增多。2004 年正月初一，慧空有幸随和尚到陕西扶风法门寺，没想到从这一天起，就被安立为侍者，从此，便有更多的机会亲近和尚了！在这个过程中，慧空不自觉地被和尚的德香熏染，仰慕之心日盛，对和尚的功德亦慢慢有些体会。

2004 年 7 月，法门寺网站改版，负责人王玉平找到慧空，希望慧空能为网站提供和尚简介。慧空觉得这件事要认真对待，于是查阅了当时一些网站、报刊、杂志对和尚的报道，发现不仅篇数较少，而且内容有些陈旧，若是把这些资料简单地组织一下放在新改版的网站上，显得有些单薄，不够充实。此时慧空正好在观阅、学习诸大善知识传记，备受启发与加持，遂于 2004 年 7 月 3 日开始动笔起草和尚简介，至 7 月 6 日完成初稿，写有 8,570 字。

During the process, besides referring to previous reports, I added what I saw, heard and contemplated about Master in recent years. Master returned to Famen Monastery in November, 2004, where I presented him with a draft of the introduction. He was very pleased and edited it personally.

Since 2007, four amendments and supplements were made on *Stories*: February 3rd— April 18th, 2007; April 7th—September 27th, 2009; February 27th—September 14th, 2010; October 5th, 2011—February 6th, 2012.

After the four revisions, the total number of Chinese characters in *Stories* had increased from 8,570 to over 47,000. It is important to note that during the fourth revision, besides some supplements, the volunteers at the Translation Center of Beijing Longquan Monastery made great resolve to translate the *Stories* into English and made it a Chinese-English version, providing more opportunities for foreigners to know about the Venerable Master. In February 2011, they started to plan and translate the *Stories* and finished the first draft in March 2011. Then there were rounds of discussions, revisions and proofreading. For the completion of a good English version, they had made great efforts and encountered many setbacks. However, faith led them break through all kinds of difficulties. Eventually, till February 6th, 2012, the final version was ready and more than 50 volunteers and foreign friends had participated in this joint effort. I would like to take this opportunity to express my sincere gratitude and heart-felt rejoice in their dedication. Their devoted contribution and earnest attitudes are greatly appreciated.

I am a person with little talent and knowledge, unable to write elegantly. It is with the Venerable Master's blessings, the help from many other venerables including Ven. Xianzhen and the support of many lay people that this book has come into being. I cannot thank them enough for their help. Furthermore, I must express my gratitude to Professor Yang Chaoguang of the University of International Business and Economics who found time to write a preface for this book and participated in the review of the English version.

However, although this book has gone through many revisions, it must have some oversights and omissions. Any comments or corrections from mentors, esteemed Buddhists and readers are sincerely appreciated!

写作过程中，慧空除了参考前人对和尚的报道外，还将亲近和尚的所见所闻所思也一并融入文中。 2004 年 11 月左右，和尚回法门寺，慧空便把写好的简介初稿呈给和尚审阅。和尚阅后很欢喜，亲自进行了修改。

从 2007 年开始，慧空先后对《侧记》进行了四次修改和增补，其时间分别是：2007 年 2 月 3 日至 4 月 18 日；2009 年 4 月 7 日至 9 月 27 日；2010 年 2 月 27 日至 9 月 14 日；2011 年 10 月 5 日至 2012 年 2 月 6 日。

经过四次修订，《侧记》由初稿的 8,570 字增加到 47,000 多字。对于第四次修订，除了新增一些内容外，特别值得一提的是，北京龙泉寺翻译中心的义工发善愿，将《侧记》翻译成英文，形成中英文对照版，为外国有缘人提供更多了解和尚的机会。2011 年 2 月，他们开始规划并着手翻译《侧记》。到 2011 年 3 月，初稿基本完成。随后他们又进行了多次讨论、修改、审校。为了这篇文稿的翻译，他们付出了很多努力，也碰到了不少难题。但，信念让他们突破了各种困难。至 2012 年 2 月 6 日终稿完成，前后参与的义工和外国友人五十余人。在此，慧空对他们致以衷心的感谢与随喜，并由衷赞叹他们至诚的发心和认真的态度。

慧空才疏学浅，文笔浅陋，本文的完成主要来自于师长的加持，同时，也得到贤振法师等众多法师和居士的鼎力相助，慧空不胜感激！在此要特别感恩对外经济贸易大学的杨潮光教授拨冗写序并参与译稿审校！

本文虽经反复斟酌修改，但疏漏之处仍在所难免，还望诸位师长、大德、善信给予指点、校正，慧空感恩不尽！

I hope that everyone who reads the book can share the joy and benefit of the Dharma, that the nation enjoys prosperity and peace, that every living being enjoys a good life, and that the Dharma ever persists and Buddhism increasingly flourishes.

Shi Huikong

At Translation Center, Beijing Longquan Monastery

February 8th, 2012

愿诸见闻者，同沾法喜，同沐法恩！

愿国泰民安，风调雨顺，众生吉祥！

愿正法久住，佛日增辉，法缘广布！

释慧空

2012 年 2 月 8 日

于北京龙泉寺翻译中心

图书在版编目（CIP）数据

学诚大和尚侧记 = Stories of Ven. Master Xuecheng ：汉英对照 / 释慧空著.
—北京：中国物资出版社，2012.2
ISBN 978-7-5047-4151-6

Ⅰ.①学… Ⅱ.①释… Ⅲ.①学诚－生平事迹－汉、英 Ⅳ.①B949.92

中国版本图书馆CIP数据核字（2012）第015591号

策划编辑	初景波		**责任印制**	方朋远	
责任编辑	白 柠		**责任校对**	孙会香 杨小静	

出版发行 中国物资出版社

社　　址　北京市丰台区南四环西路188号5区20楼　　邮政编码：100070

电　　话　010－52227568（发行部）　　　　010－52227588转307（总编室）
　　　　　010－68589540（读者服务部）　　010－52227588转305（质检部）

网　　址　http://www.clph.cn

经　　销　新华书店

印　　刷　北京京都六环印刷厂

书　　号　ISBN 978-7-5047-4151-6 / B · 0407

开　　本　787mm×1092mm　1/16

印　　张　17　　　　　　　　　　　　　　版　　次　2012年2月第1版

字　　数　197千字　　　　　　　　　　　印　　次　2012年2月第1次印刷

印　　数　00001—12000册　　　　　　　定　　价　46.00元